*Members of the Confederate battalion of the National Civil War Association.*

*A wartime photo of Sunday morning mass at the camp of the 69th N.Y.*

# PRAISE FOR *Civil War Woodworking*

## MARLEN KEMMET

"A century before the advent of precision power tools with laser guides and micro-adjustments, projects were made with much simpler tools and just as much pride and passion as they are today. Accomplished woodworking author and Civil War reenactor A.J. Hamler shares a host of historically rooted Civil War woodworking projects and processes to bring these period pieces back to life. From ammo boxes to an officer's field desk, Hamler provides a thoroughly researched look at how you can make these pieces yourself with authenticity."

—Marlen Kemmet, managing editor for *WOOD* Magazine

## PHIL MCBRIDE

"A.J. Hamler is an avid Civil War reenactor and a professional-level wood craftsman and writer. Military and civilian reenactors who strive for period-correct accuracy will relish the information on 19th century nails, tools, stencils, and the wood itself. Civil War reenactors will be glad to have do-able projects that will add authenticity to their camp furniture and period impressions. This practical and attractive book won't be gathering dust on my bookshelf, but it likely will get smudged with sawdust while I try my hand at building Mr. Hamler's projects."

—Phil McBride, The Alamo Rifles, San Antonio, Texas; writer for *Camp Chase Gazette*

## DOUG STOWE

"As a woodworker and writer, I am interested in seeing others find pleasure in woodworking similar to my own. As a teacher, I am interested in the ways woodworking can help subjects like history come to life with greater depth and significance. This book appeals to both interests."

—Doug Stowe, wisdomofhands.blogspot.com; author of *Rustic Furniture Basics*

## KERRY PIERCE

"A.J. Hamler's book *Civil War Woodworking* offers reenactors detailed construction info about many buildable accoutrements of period conflict, but non-reenactors may value the book just as much for its depiction of two fascinating worlds: the world of the soldiers who fought in the 1860s conflict and the world of the modern American reenactors."

—Kerry Pierce, author of *Pleasant Hill Shaker Furniture*

## KIM PERLOTTO

"A.J. Hamler is a longtime friend, a passionate reenactor, and an accomplished carpenter. Putting those qualities together, he describes great woodworking projects that make your camp more comfortable and more authentic. His is a fine contribution to the hobby, and he makes each of these projects simple, accurate, and interesting. My compliments to A.J. for helping us all make perfect camp and garrison equipage for ourselves."

—Kim Perlotto, 8th Regiment Connecticut Volunteer Infantry, Company A

*Confederate prisoners being held after the battle of Gettysburg, July, 1863.*

# CIVIL WAR WOODWORKING

*17 Authentic Projects*
*for Woodworkers and Reenactors*

A.J. HAMLER

Linden Publishing
Fresno

*To Ben and Barbara Bova—It didn't turn out quite the way we thought, but without their help, encouragement and friendship I wouldn't be a full-time writer today.*

To order another copy of this book, please call
**1-800-345-4447.**

Editor: Kent Sorsky
Cover design: James Goold
Photography: A.J. Hamler, except where noted.
Design and layout: Maura J. Zimmer

ISBN 978-1-933502-28-1

Printed in China on acid-free paper.

135798642

Woodworking is inherently dangerous. Your safety is your responsibility.
Neither Linden Publishing nor the author assume any responsibility for any injuries or accidents.
Several photographs in this book depict the usage of woodworking machinery where the safety guards
have been removed. The guards were removed for clarity. *We urge you to utilize all available
safety equipment and follow all recommended safety procedures when woodworking.*

Library of Congress Cataloging-in-Publication Data

Hamler, A. J. (Anthony J.), 1951-

Civil War woodworking : 17 authentic projects for woodworkers and reenactors / by A.J. Hamler.

  p. cm.

ISBN 978-1-933502-28-1 (pbk. : alk. paper)

1. Woodwork--Amateurs' manuals. 2. Woodwork--United States--History--19th century. 3. United States--History--Civil War, 1861-1865--Equipment and supplies. 4. United States. Army--Military life--History--19th century. 5. Confederate States of America. Army--Military life--History--19th century. 6. Historical reenactments--United States. I. Title.

  TT185.H319 2009

684'.08--dc22

                                                                    2009015288

# Acknowledgments

I've been a woodworker for a long time, and although I've studied the Civil War for many years and have picked up a large volume of historical lore, my knowledge of the period still has gaps—many, many gaps. For that reason, this book would not have been possible without the expertise, information, suggestions and knowledge of several people, many of whom I'm fortunate to call friends. In no particular order, my thanks to the following:

Joe Cress, of Logan Creek Designs, was extremely helpful with historical information on field desks. He should know something about them, as he's been making expertly crafted reproductions of field desks for 15 years based on originals belonging to Stonewall Jackson, J.E.B. Stuart, and Robert E. Lee.

Ken Weaver, of K&P Weaver, is a fellow member of the 27th Connecticut Volunteer Infantry, and has been a Civil War sutler for many years. I bought my first Federal uniform from K&P 15 years ago, and I appreciate Ken's insights on authentic lanterns and mirrors. K&P recently shifted emphasis to uniforms and equipment for 19th-century baseball. His Web site is *www.baseballamericaspastime.com*.

Bob Flexner, author of *Understanding Wood Finishing*, has been a woodworking friend and colleague for several years. His help and advice on 19th-century finishing details was invaluable.

Larry Bickett, Production Controller at the Tremont Nail Co., provided tons of background on the cut-nail industry in the 1800s. His company still makes cut nails of the same patterns (and on some of the same machines) from back then.

The original A.T. Hanks hardtack crate I used as the basis for the stencil in Chapter 4 was on display at the Museum of Connecticut History in Hartford, Conn. Dean Nelson, Museum Administrator, helped me with several details on that particular crate.

Bob Gregory, who I "met" online while doing Civil War research, was a big help on both hardtack crates and ammo boxes. In fact, it was Gregory who tipped me off about the location of that original A.T. Hanks crate.

Will Dunniway, Collodion Photographer, produces incredible images of modern reenactors that look like they were taken during the war. He graciously allowed me to use several of his images for this book. See more of his work at *www.collodion-artist.com*.

Dana Martin Batory, author of Vintage Woodworking Machinery, is another woodworking buddy. I've picked his brain more times than I can think of on the subject of old woodworking equipment. He provided the 1856 catalog image of the industrial planer appearing in Chapter 2.

And last, but not least, my thanks to Louise Parsons for the old shovel.

# A note on the period photographs

All of the original Civil War photos used in this book were created using a process called wet-plate collodion photography. Although invented in England only 10 years earlier by Frederick Scott Archer, by the time of the Civil War the process had swept the world. Literally thousands of collodion images were made during the war, including those from the Library of Congress and National Archives that are featured throughout this book. As the name implies, the photographic plates used in collodion work are wet, so the images must be developed and processed immediately after photos are taken.

Also featured in this book are modern photos of contemporary Civil War reenactors made by Will Dunniway. As with his 19th-century counterparts, Dunniway must carry what amounts to an entire photo studio with him, including all the necessary chemicals.

Dunniway, a 35-year professional photographer who has devoted the past two decades to collodion work, recently published a collection of his work, *Will Dunniway the Collodion Photographer*. The 152-page book includes 140 images spanning historical subjects from the 19th century to the present. His Web site, *www.collodion-artist.com*, features numerous photos from his portfolio.

*Above: Contemporary self-portrait by collodion photographer Will Dunniway.*

# *Table of Contents*

This simple bench, a mainstay for seating for centuries in both civilian and
military life, is easy to make and very practical for an army on the move.

Hardtack crackers fed the armies of both North and South, and the empty crates were
recycled for camp use for storage and seating. They can even be turned into coolers.

These boxes were common camp items, used for storage and seating. They're an essential
storage item for reenactors—or anyone needed a sturdy, authentic container.

Solid and utilitarian, this sturdy camp table folds flat for storage or transport.

The portable saw of its day, it's perfect for both the 19th and 21st centuries.

Using only eight wooden components, this simple scissors-style stool can be
made with a variety of commonly available materials.

*Reenactors from various units pose for a patriotic photo by collodion photographer Will Dunniway.*

*Part One*

# GETTING STARTED

*Reenactor Jim Bob Thompson of the 14th Tenn. Co. H relaxes in camp.*

# Chapter 1:
# STEPPING BACK IN TIME

*It's hot, although not as hot as it was the last two days. The rains last night cooled things down somewhat, but looking down the hill toward the line of trees the sweat still trickles from beneath my forage cap. I can feel the dampness of my shirt beneath my sack coat, and my palms are sweaty on the Springfield rifle in my hands. The barrel shows rust spots already; I'll have to clean it good tonight.*

*We lay flat on the ground, our heads downhill. The rest of my regiment spreads out on either side of me, each man wincing slightly every time the line of artillery to our rear continues its barrage on the tree line. The Rebs couldn't possibly attack our position here, and yet the commanding general insists on hammering those trees, the batteries behind us firing with a steady boom–boom–boom every few seconds.*

*Suddenly, there's movement at the edge of the trees as thousands of men move into the open. They stand in formation as their commanders address them, and with a flare of bugles, drums and swords waved in our direction, they step off en masse toward the base of the hill below us. Are they mad to attack our entrenched position that so completely commands the field of fire? And yet, as they come out of the trees, I see they are thousands, and they march steadfastly toward us. Even the artillery shells falling in their number do nothing to slow their forward progress. These are brave men, and I silently nod my head in respect for their courage even as the order to rise up is given.*

*Although difficult to see through the smoke, there are more than 5,000 reenactors in the field taking part in a portion of the battle of Antietam.*

*I get to my feet and dress to the man on my right, standing at attention. They draw nearer, and I can begin to make out details: a hat here, a kerchief around a neck there. One man wears no coat, while another behind him is hatless. A man to his left limps, but keeps up with his pards. Their faces are dirty, and their brows glisten with sweat.*

*Our commander shouts. We stiffen further, dressing our lines. Our hands tighten on our rifles.*

*"Ready!"*

*Automatically I shift to the T-stance, porting my musket to the right and forward. This is it, I think. My eyes settle on the man with the kerchief.*

*"Aim!"*

*A hundred rifles rattle as they are simultaneously cocked and brought to the shoulder. I train my rifle on the man in the kerchief, waiting. The man is clearer now, exhausted from the heat and the trek up the hill. He doesn't fire. None of the men advancing on us are firing. Yet.*

*Our eyes meet, still a hundred yards apart. He has somehow singled me out just as I have him. He sees me and, more importantly, that I'm aiming at him. He nods in a matter-of-fact way, and presses forward, lifting his Enfield toward me.*

*I've never taken blood on the field. Can I do this now, can I follow through on what is my duty and honor at this time of our nation's greatest need? I don't have time to answer my own uncertainty as the command is given.*

*"Fire!"*

*Still looking into the man's eyes, I fire. The combined roar of the battalion is deafening, the white cloud of smoke from the rifles pungent. I feel a sting on my left cheek from a tiny fragment of percussion cap sent flying from the musket at my left. The sudden sting sharpens my view of the man in the kerchief, who— never taking his eyes off me—falls to his knees. He gazes at me a moment, then drops to the ground on top of his musket. The advancing men of his brigade part and pass around him.*

# Today's fascination with the Civil War

An excerpt from a soldier's memoirs, or maybe an eyewitness account of one violent day in 1863? Well, not quite.

I've taken a few literary liberties in the narrative, but it's essentially an accurate description of a staging of the famous Pickett's Charge on the third day of the battle of Gettysburg. I was portraying a Union corporal with the 27th Connecticut reenactment unit, and was part of a larger Federal force numbering in the thousands arrayed before a line of dozens of cannon. Coming up that hill were thousands of Confederate reenactors, nearly as many as took part in the real Pickett's charge on July 3, 1863.

And, yes, that Rebel really did "take a hit" when I fired.

*Members of the 2nd Va. Cavalry take part in 2004 funeral ceremonies for the crew of the Confederate submarine* H.L. Hunley, *which was recovered in 2000.*

No one knows exactly how many reenactors took part in this reenactment—the 135th anniversary Gettysburg event in 1997—because the number of participants far exceeded the organizers' expectations. Registration for these events is pretty strict, but by this third day of the event the number of registered participants and unregistered walk-ons was so large that organizers more or less gave up. Since then, estimates have ranged from 15,000 reenactors taking part to more than 20,000, and while few agree on the actual number of participants, the event is widely considered the largest reenactment ever staged.

Reenacting, obviously, is very popular. Estimates of the total number of active Civil War reenactors have varied over the years. In 1986—the beginning of the boom years for reenacting—*Time* magazine estimated there were as many as 50,000 reenactors. Ken Burns' *The Civil War* on PBS a few years later, followed by popular movies like *Gettysburg*, *Cold Mountain* and *Glory*, have helped to periodically revive interest.

*Reenactors stage a crucial point of the construction of the* H.L. Hunley *in this modern wet-plate collodion image.*

It may surprise you to learn that almost all major world conflicts have a reenactment following. The American Revolution, both World Wars, even Korea and Vietnam have their share of reenacting devotees. None, however, can match the numbers (and sheer enthusiasm) of those dedicated to the Civil War.

When you consider how demanding reenacting is, enthusiasm is a requirement. The temperature at the Gettysburg event I described above was in the mid-90s for all but the final day, and each reenactor wore a full wool uniform and carried between 20 and 40 pounds of gear. From the time we left camp to the time Pickett's Charge was over, we'd covered several miles on foot. The uniforms and equipment—leather accoutrements, musket, footwear, etc.—can cost between $1,200 and $2,000 (or more) depending on the impression portrayed. It's not unusual for a reenactor to drive 500 or more miles to attend a large event, and then camp out with minimal comforts for several days once he's there.

Maybe "enthusiasm" isn't the right word.

## Authenticity and the reenacting community

So why do they do it? Reasons vary, but almost every reenactor will cite two reasons: First, it's a heck of a lot of fun. It probably harkens back to a time when every young boy played cops and robbers, except now all the toys—including the guns—are real. It's a weekend getaway from jobs, paying bills and responsibilities. It's hanging out with a bunch of guys who share your interests. It's making loud noises and getting dirty. What's not to like?

The second, more important reason, is a love of history and helping to bring history to life for others, hence the term "Living History." While some reenactors prefer the action and excitement of the battle scenarios ("burning powder" as it's called), most enjoy interacting with the public and take pride in sharing their knowledge of the period. To that end, reenactors work very hard to present an accurate "impression" when it comes to their appearance and gear. Many do endless amounts of online and library research to learn as much as possible about the history of the mid-19th century, the soldier's life, and every aspect of his uniform and equipment. The vast majority have a high regard for authenticity, but within the ranks there's a wide variation on authenticity levels.

Authenticity-wise, reenactors are divided into three main groups:

**Farb**—"Farb" is a derisive term coined by reenactors to describe those who make little effort at being authentic or period-correct. The typical Farb reenactor is easy to spot. He'll be wearing work boots or hiking shoes instead of 19th-century brogans. Jarring anachronisms like wristwatches, modern glasses and even sunglasses are common in their apparel, while brightly colored plastic coolers, soda cans and cell phones are glaringly visible in camp. There's almost no chance that a Farb would make an effort to adopt a 19th-century persona to present a first-person impression of a true Confederate or Union soldier.

**Mainstream**—By far the largest group, Mainstream reenactors generally present a fairly accurate impression when in view of the public. Uniforms, equipment and camp settings are usually authentic in a visual sense, and many Mainstreamers go out of their way to incorporate additional period gear into their public impressions. Mainstream reenacting units are among the largest in the hobby, and those units with strong leadership encourage authenticity at all times when dealing with the public. At the end of the

*Reenacting is a multigenerational hobby. This father and son, members of the 27th Conn., enjoy a beautiful autumn day in Falls Village, Conn.*

day when the camps are closed to the public, however, authenticity rules relax for some: Guys who did without glasses during the day may put them back on, coolers are retrieved from hiding spots, cell phones emerge to check in with family at home. There's a huge variation in the mainstream category when it comes to authenticity. Some groups are very lax with few hard and fast rules, while many are quite strict regarding what's permitted; most fall somewhere in the middle.

**Hardcore**—These guys take authenticity to the extreme, often going for full immersion. While a Mainstreamer may wear modern Fruit-of-the-Looms underneath a perfectly authentic uniform, a Hardcore is wearing 100% period-correct under drawers. Most leave everything from the 21st century in their cars for the weekend, and subsist entirely on what they carry into the camps on their backs. Their uniforms and equipment are among the most expensive around, with every tiny detail enviably correct to the 1860s. (Some Hardcores have earned the derisive moniker "stitch counter" for literally

*The typical campaign-style camp offers few comforts. Note the lack of stools, lanterns and other items that soldiers would not have carried on the march.*

counting the number of hand-sewn stitches in a buttonhole.) A large number of Hardcores adopt a period persona at the beginning of an event, and don't come out of character till the weekend is over. Their dedication to authenticity is incredible.

While those are the three main groups, there are a few gray areas among them, plus some additional subgroups. "Campaigners" and "Progressives" straddle the line between mainstream and hardcore, for example. Civilian reenactors eschew military impressions, and concentrate on accurate portrayals of the general public of the 1860s. Other reenactors opt for impressions of other walks of life from the period, such as clergy, journalists, photographers and the like. All (except Farbs) strive for authenticity in their appearance.

## Defining authenticity: What is "period-correct?"

It may seem that when it comes to authenticity reenactors concentrate on their clothing, and because their "costume" encompasses the largest percentage of their visual impression, that's mostly true. However, the goal of authenticity extends past clothing to all personal effects. For the soldier, it includes leather gear, accoutrements such as cartridge box and haversack, and weaponry. Although today's reproduction muskets are fairly true to the originals, many reenactors take extra steps to make them more authentic, like grinding off modern manufacturers' markings or stripping the wooden stocks and recoating them with a more period-correct finish.

So, what exactly does "period-correct" mean in this context? The term simply means that a modern reproduction item—anything from a Confederate slouch hat to a Federal cannon—should be made using the same materials that would have been used in the 1860s. For uniforms, that means all-natural

*Although this 1861 Springfield is fairly accurate, that serial number and some other markings are pure 21st century and not period-correct.*

fabrics must be used: cotton, wool, linen, and silk are fine; polyester, nylon, acrylic, and spandex are not. Further, construction methods should be as close to the original methods used at the time. Using uniforms as an example once more, fabric and stitching should conform to 1860s standards. Machine sewing was common during the period, but for the most part only straight stitching is acceptable, with all modern stitching such as "zig-zag" and others strictly avoided.

Authentic reenactors also pay attention to regional specifics when it comes to their gear. Using clothing one last time as an example, a reenactor portraying a Union soldier from New York City may be period-correct wearing a machine-sewn shirt (even machined buttonholes, although not common, had appeared in larger industrial cities of the North during the war). The uniform of a Rebel soldier hailing from rural Alabama, however, may be period-correct only if totally hand-sewn.

I've used clothing as an example up to this point because it's the most obvious aspect of a reenactor's appearance, but the same considerations extend to woodworking items used as part of a reenactor's gear or "kit." A wooden camp stool, lantern or even a discarded shipping crate must also be as period-correct as possible.

As with clothing, a large portion of achieving authenticity in constructing wooden items is to simply avoid modern materials and methods. For example, no wooden item from the 1860s should be made of plywood. Although sheet material made of individual wooden plies dates back to ancient Egypt, the modern method of creating plywood by laminating several layers of thin veneers didn't arrive till the mid- to late 19th century. And not only was that plywood extremely rare in common use, it was vastly different from what is available today. (Plywood made today wouldn't be period-correct for early 20th-century reproductions either, for that matter.) Other materials to be avoided include Phillip's-head screws, wire nails, polyurethane varnish and latex paint. Further, metal fasteners of the period were limited for the most part to iron, mild steel, copper and brass. Aluminum nails or stainless steel screws simply weren't used.

There was mass production of furniture and other wooden items during the period, but a lot was still hand-made. Lumber frequently came from large facilities where some surprisingly modern equipment was already in use—large circular and vertical saws turned out dimensional lumber, although the surfaces of that lumber were not as smooth as what you'll find at the local home center. (It also wasn't the same size as what you buy today. A 2x4 during the Civil War measured 2" thick and 4" wide; today a 2x4 measures only 1½" by 3½".)

When those wooden items were made, they were made with hand power, even in the large furniture factories. Portable circular saws, routers, pneumatic nailers, pad sanders and cordless drills were still more than half a century away. Instead, handsaws, hand planes, hammers, scrapers and bit-and-brace setups took their places, respectively. Often, our modern power tools leave different types of milling marks on wood surfaces that are not period-correct. A handsaw makes a very different-looking cut on the end of a board than a circular saw does, so anyone attempting to recreate period-correct wooden reproductions must take these into consideration, too.

I'll cover all of these aspects in greater detail in the next chapter, as well as in the individual projects as needed.

## How authentic can your project really be?

Civil War reenactors are an opinionated bunch, and the merits of one method of authenticity versus another are frequently, and hotly, debated around the campfire, in periodicals and on the various online forums devoted to the hobby. I have no

*Workers in an ambulance shop, circa 1865.*

doubt that many of my conclusions on the nature of the projects in this book will spark heated discussions both pro and con. However, I suspect that none of my opinions will be as inflammatory as the one that follows:

I don't believe it's possible to make a 100%-authentic reproduction of *any* historical item.

There are many reasons for this. For one thing, materials produced today simply are not the same as those produced in the 1860s. Commonly available "over-the-counter" wood or metal materials are made far differently than they were then. Some may come close—or can be reworked to be closer—but they're still different. A number of specialty suppliers have, for the last few decades, dedicated themselves to re-creating supplies for Living History customers that approximate as closely as possible the originals. This is most easily done with fabrics, and there are numerous vendors who make available cloth that has been woven to the same specifications, with the right fiber mix, and on similar looms to those used back then.

Likewise, metal formulations are far different today. Even the steel used in otherwise period-correct cut steel nails is, of economic and practical necessity, a different formulation. The same thing holds true for screws and rivets.

You may be thinking at this point that this issue doesn't apply to wood, but you'd be wrong. The basic pine board you bought last week at Home Depot is not an exact match for a pine board of identical dimensions milled in 1864. For one thing, almost all wood milled today is from new-growth forests; in fact, it's most likely cut from trees grown in the last few decades specifically to produce that lumber. That wasn't the case 145 years ago, when the vast majority of lumber came from existing old-growth forests, and old-growth wood simply doesn't match new-growth wood. It may be so close that only an experienced forester could tell the difference, but it's still not the same.

I'll grant that it might be possible to salvage wood from, say, a 145-year-old barn as a material source. Then, using original antique hand tools, and some original nails salvaged from a 145-year-old house, and using only 19th-century construction techniques, you might just be able to put together something that would fool the casual eye… but not the eye of an expert.

The best you'll be able to achieve is a compromise, and the question then becomes how much compromise you're willing to accept. Fortunately, reenactors are accustomed to compromise. For example, battles can feel extraordinarily real when you're taking part, and I tried to express that in my opening scenario describing the reenactment of Pickett's Charge at the 135th Gettysburg event. However, we—all 15,000+ of us—willingly made numerous period-incorrect compromises during that battle. For example, safety rules forbade us from removing bayonets from scabbards while on the field (some event organizers don't even allow bayonets to be carried). When soldiers are closer than a few score yards from each other, even though we're using blanks all rifles must be elevated for safety when fired; that is, we shot over each other's heads. Volunteers in period clothing were never far away, carrying water for anyone who needed it. On a personal level, any reenactor taking prescription medications didn't skip it that morning just because they were pretending to be 19th-century soldiers, and quite a few were wearing sunscreen. Not a one of these modern compromises is period-correct, but by the same token none of them diminished the historical experience.

LIBRARY OF CONGRESS

*A member of the 31st Pa. Infantry, camped near Ft. Slocum in Washington D.C., appears ready to do some in-the-field woodworking.*

# *What to expect from these projects*

I've done a lot of research for all the projects in this book, and I'm personally satisfied they are as authentic as they can practically be. For each project, I'll guide you through the construction, pointing out the most correct way at each step. On occasion, I'll also suggest some compromise steps, materials, or techniques that, although perhaps not quite 100% authentic, will still yield an authentic-looking reproduction.

For example, the Ammunition Box project in Chapter 5 incorporates optional cleats on the underside of the lid. The originals weren't made with lid cleats, but since it's likely you'll use the box for storage purposes, you'll need a way to keep the lid in one piece that easily stays on. Whether to include the cleats is up to you, but I'll describe the project both ways and leave it to you to decide how much of a compromise you're willing to make. In most cases, the compromises I'll suggest aren't visible to the casual eye, so they won't detract from an overall authentic appearance. Those cleats are a good example: When the lid is on the box, no one can see them.

Finally, there's another important difference between the way many of these projects were built originally and how you'll probably want to make them today. Back then, a lot of these items—hardtack crates, ammo boxes, camp benches and tables, etc.—were made for temporary use only. Hardtack crates, for example, were the Big Mac containers of their day: They were made for a single purpose, and once empty were intended to be discarded. A bench may have been made in camp, and then simply left behind when the army moved. Further, it cost only pennies to make most of those disposable wooden things.

Conversely, it will cost you more to make these projects (plus, the money comes out of *your* pocket and not the army's), and you'll want these things to last a while, especially if you plan to use them in the field. I understand this and have designed some of these projects accordingly to be a bit sturdier than their ancestors. Still, I'll point out anything I've done to make them sturdier, giving you the option of doing it that way or not.

So, are you ready? Grab your tools and let's take a trip to the 19th century.

# Chapter 2:
## BRINGING THE PAST TO LIFE

This book is not intended to be a tutorial on woodworking skills and techniques. For that I refer you to any of the many excellent titles available on the subject from Linden Publishing and others. As I describe the steps of each project, I'll assume a certain amount of experience with common woodworking tools and techniques.

Further, this is not a book about using antique tools. All the tools used for the projects—whether power tools or hand tools—are modern ones. However, I will vary the tools used for similar techniques to give you options on how to make the projects based on the tools you own. For example, to make a mortise-and-tenon joint, you can create the mortise in a single step with a benchtop mortiser. Or, lacking a dedicated mortiser, you can make a mortise in two steps with a drill press and hand chisel. I'll describe both and let you decide which is best for you. Likewise,

*A group of woodworkers in 1865 show off the tools of their trade.*

tongue-and-groove joints can be made on either the table saw or the router table, so I'll mention both options as appropriate.

## Woodworking in the 19th century

It may be helpful to start by discussing how woodworking was done 145 years ago, especially as it applies to the projects in this book. Woodworking and woodworkers back then, excepting the lack of powered equipment and the limitations of available materials, were not all that different from today. Most of the basic materials we have today (with notable exceptions) existed then. Take away the power, and most of the tools were similar. The joinery they used then, with the exception of joinery specific to modern tools such as biscuit joiners, was exactly the same.

Wood in large cities and industrial areas, in both the North and South, came from mills not unlike those we have today. Even lumber mills in less-populated areas often turned out lumber and building materials milled and cut in quantity using industrial belt-driven saws powered by water or, less often, by steam. The saws themselves were similar to modern ones. The circular saw was developed in England in 1777—it was dubbed a "saw bench" then—and was quickly adopted in the United States. Huge "up-and-down" saws similar in action to a sewing machine, with a reciprocating vertical blade, were used even earlier. Up-and-down saws were essentially larger, mechanized versions of pit saws, where two men—one on a sawing platform and the other below in a pit—used muscle power to cut planks. Some of these mechanized saws occupied two floors of a mill, using blades of 10' in length and more that extended to gearing below the floor.

Once cut, lumber was often surfaced and brought to final thickness with planers similar to those in use today. Records of planers go

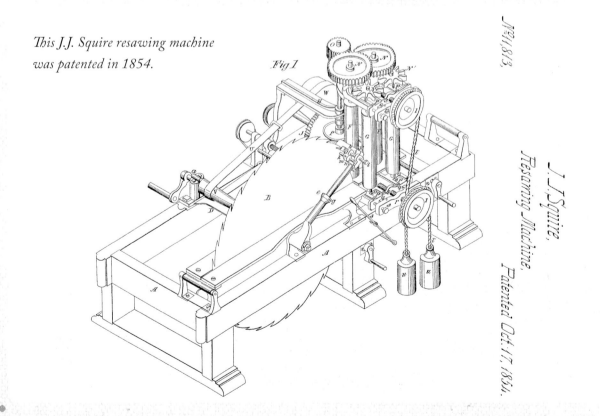

*This J.J. Squire resawing machine was patented in 1854.*

back to 1776, but the first one that operated like modern planers with cutters and stock feeders was developed by William Woodworth in Poughkeepsie, N.Y., in 1828. The 1840s, '50s and '60s saw several patents for improvements in industrial wood planers.

Wood fasteners were limited to nails, screws and rivets made of iron, mild steel, brass and copper. Galvanizing of metal to resist the elements existed, but wasn't common. Tinning iron for surface durability and protection also took place, but was not common for carpentry materials.

Molders existed in the 1860s, but were not common and were used primarily in only larger industrial areas of the North. Most moldings of the period were made by hand with a combination of hand planes using blades cut to the desired profiles.

Fine furniture of the period was made exactly as it is today: as perfectly as possible. Tables were smooth, joints fit tightly, legs were even and well-formed. Utility woodworking, on the other hand, varied widely. Boxes for shipping and storage were often made from very rough wood, and often with a minimum of joinery. Butt joints were commonplace, nails were the most common fastener, and nobody cared if you could see the nails in the finished item.

Likewise, utility items not intended as fine furniture were often far cruder than today's standards. Stools used around the home and farm were generally plain, and not always particularly smooth. If they had a finish coat of any kind, it was likely a simple drying oil, such as boiled linseed oil, shellac or paint. Just as often, simple furniture was left unfinished. Staining lighter-colored woods to imitate more exotic species wasn't common for most simple furniture and wooden items.

*A typical planer of the period might resemble this one offered in the 1856 edition of the J.A. Fay & Co. catalog.*

DANA MARTIN BATORY

DANIELS'S IMPROVED PLANING MACHINE, WITH REED'S FEED MOTION.

# Materials and stock considerations

## WOOD

For many of the reproduction projects in this book, regular off-the-shelf lumber from your local home center will work fine as long as you keep a few things in mind. I'll give specific details on this for each project, but here are some considerations.

The most common wood used for just about all utility items in the 19th century was softwood that came from species in the spruce, pine and fir families. Today we call this category "SPF lumber," and it's what most building materials are made from; I'll use the term frequently throughout the projects. Lumber today is shipped everywhere, but the most commonly available SPF lumber in your area will vary depending on what grows locally. This was even truer then. In your reproductions, keep in mind where the article's intended use would have been. For example, if you're making the Five-Board Bench project in Chapter 3 for use in, say, a Gettysburg scenario, the bench would probably have been made with the white pine common in the North. Make the same bench for a South Carolina scenario, and it's more likely to have been yellow pine.

Almost all simple furniture constructed in the field—meaning items made by the soldiers themselves—would be made from softwood in the SPF families. It was available everywhere, easy to harvest, lightweight, of low density, easy to cut, and very easy to work. Most field-made items were built for temporary use and often abandoned when the army moved, so there was no need to make them particularly sturdy, long-lasting or even good looking. Raw edges and rough surfaces were common. Sometimes, soldiers would acquire wooden items from homes and farms that were made there or by carpenters in nearby towns or cities. SPF lumber was used in these items too, but now you would also begin to see more use of hardwoods like oak, hickory, maple, walnut, poplar and cherry. The construction details of these items would be a bit better as well. And, naturally, items intended as finer furniture would usually be of hardwood, and would incorporate more intricate joinery and finishing techniques.

Of course, there were no rules so any item could be made of any wood that was available locally back then. The amount of detail the carpenter used in the joinery was limited only by his talent, and the tools and time available to him.

As I suggested in the previous chapter, period-correctness and authenticity for reproduction items often depends less on what you use than what you *don't* use. If it didn't exist then, don't use it now if you're going for a high level of authenticity. This rules out all forms of what's commonly called engineered lumber. Plywood, particleboard, hardboard, oriented-strand board (OSB), medium-density fiberboard (MDF) and, obviously, all plastics and synthetics should be avoided. Now, if you're willing to make some compromises, some of those materials *might* be useable in certain circumstances. I'll address that in more detail in a few moments.

Keep in mind that lumber in the 1860s didn't look quite the same as lumber you'll buy today. For one thing, lumber was produced in sizes that were actually accurate back then. If you bought a piece of 1x10 pine, for example, it measured no less than 1" thick and 10" wide. A 1x10 from your local Lowe's or Home Depot measures only ¾" thick and 9¼" wide. What's more, that board you get today will be perfectly smooth; boards back then were far rougher. Sure, a good craftsman could make a piece of furniture mirror-smooth, but many utility items like simple stools or shipping crates were made with lumber that was quite rough. For that reason, avoid the temptation to sand everything to death.

*The home-center oak board in the foreground is ¾" thick and has been planed very smooth. The oak board from a specialty lumber dealer is slightly more than 1" thick, and although evenly planed has rough surfaces on all four sides.*

You can make smooth wood a little bit rougher by wetting it. Do this with a sponge, wiping it across flat exposed surfaces (avoid end grain). You want the wood surface to be thoroughly wet, but don't use so much water that it's dripping and running everywhere. A good wipe-down will do. When the water dries, you'll find that it has raised the grain somewhat to give what once was a perfectly smooth surface a rougher texture. Once you get it this way, don't sand it.

Finally, with regard to wood sizes you must realize that wood used in carpentry came in a wide range of thicknesses. Today, virtually all lumber for sale at home centers (with the exception of construction lumber) comes in a single thickness: ¾", which is why almost all the camp furniture you see at reenactments or offered for sale by sutlers (sellers of Civil War items for reenactors) is this thickness. As a result, ¾" lumber is grossly over-represented in the hobby. (That's a term you'll hear me use throughout this book.) Now, it's perfectly authentic to use ¾"-thick lumber for these projects and, for the sake of practicality and uniformity, in the material list measurements I'll use it for several of the projects included here—but considering how over-represented it is my advice is to use another

thickness whenever possible. You won't find thicker boards at a home center other than construction lumber, but a larger lumber supplier should have an abundance of 1" boards in stock, and may also have a quantity of 2" and larger stock as well. These larger lumber sources probably list their lumber in "quarter" sizes where each size is named in ¼" increments. In this measurement system a ¾" board is described as 3/4 lumber (pronounced "three-four"), a 1" board is 4/4 (four-four), a 2" board is 8/4 (eight-four), and so on.

You can also mill your own stock from standard 2-by construction lumber. For example, to get the 1"-thick pine used for the ends of the Hardtack Crate project in Chapter 4, I bought a piece of standard 2x12 construction lumber (which is really only 1½" x 11¼") and machine-planed it down to exactly 1" thick. Of course, if the local home center is your only source of lumber, remember that the only 2-by stock they carry is SPF.

## HARDWARE AND FASTENERS

For authentic reproductions, use hardware and fasteners made only of iron, mild steel, brass and copper.

Iron was the most common material for screws, nails, locksets and hinges during the period and you should use those whenever possible. Unfortunately, most iron or steel screws, hinges and locks available today are coated with a material—usually a zinc alloy—that makes them shiny as a car bumper. This is not period-correct. Brand new iron hinges or mild steel rivets of the 1860s would be naturally shiny when made, but would quickly turn to a dull finish in use (and, in fact, were usually already dull by the time the carpenter acquired them). Modern steel hinges can stay chrome-shiny forever. You can sometimes find plain steel hinges and screws in large hardware stores, online, or from specialty suppliers, but if you're forced to use the shiny ones, consider removing the coating from the visible portion of the hinge with sandpaper before use. Same thing for screw heads.

Better yet, skip those shiny steel ones and use brass hinges and screws. Brass was less commonly used than plain iron or steel back then, but it is still period-correct for any reproduction item in this book. Modern brass hardware is often coated with a lacquer finish to retard the tarnishing process; if this is the case, remove it by soaking the hinges in paint remover before use.

It should go without saying by this point that you should only use hardware and fasteners that were available at the time. For nails, that means cut iron or steel nails only—machinery to produce the wire nails we use today began to appear in the mid-1800s, but nails of that type suitable for general carpentry were almost nonexistent during the Civil War. Cut tacks of steel, brass and copper were also

*Cut nails come in a variety of head and body styles, and in lengths up to 6".*

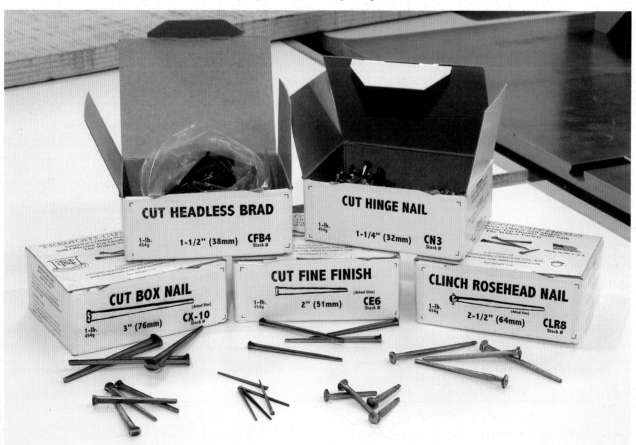

commonly used. Likewise, the only screws that existed then were slotted, with either a round-head or flat-head design. Phillip's, square-drive, star-drive or any other modern screws didn't exist, so don't use them. That goes double for those common black "drywall" screws.

Something else that should be noted is that the holes created by nails and screws weren't filled then to hide the heads; no putty, no wood filler. On some occasions for finer furniture, screws may have been hidden with wooden plugs, but the practice was not yet common. It would have been far more likely, in the case of fine furniture, to use dovetails or other joinery methods that required no visible fasteners, or for fasteners to be hidden on the underside and backs of finished pieces.

One last type of fastener should be mentioned, and that's wooden dowels. Dowels are used the same way as nails, but a pilot hole is first drilled into the wood before the dowel is driven in. Dowel fasteners were most often used to secure other forms of joinery; for example, a tenon might be pegged solidly in place by drilling a hole through the side of a mortise-and-tenon joint and driving a dowel firmly into the hole. We'll use that technique for Lt. Kelly's Camp Chair project in Chapter 9.

In the previous section on wood I promised to elaborate on a compromise that might allow you to use modern materials or fasteners in an otherwise authentic-looking project. If a modern material or fastener will not be seen in normal use, you might opt to use it, but again it all depends on how much you are willing to compromise regarding authenticity. For example, no one sees the bottom of the drawer in the Field Desk project in Chapter 10, so you could use a thin sheet of plywood for the drawer bottom instead of the solid wood I used. (For that matter, even if seen it's unlikely anyone would ever know it wasn't solid wood.) Likewise, if a screw will be covered by another material or component of the project, no one but you will know if it's a period-correct slotted steel screw or

a modern stainless-steel Phillip's screw. In both cases the modern choice would be stronger and easier to use, but would not be authentic to the period. The bottom line is deciding on how much compromise you're willing to make.

## *Tools and techniques*

### WOOD MARKINGS

As I stated earlier, this book is not about using nothing but antique tools to make the reproduction projects in the following chapters. For that matter, it's not even about using only hand tools. You're welcome to do both, of course, but my personal compromise (and that of the majority of this book's readership, I'm guessing) is to use the tools I have on hand in such a way as to create acceptably authentic and period-correct items.

However, it should be kept in mind that modern tools sometimes make different marks on wood than did the old tools. This is especially true of modern power equipment.

Few small carpentry shops in the 1860s had much, if any, woodworking machinery, especially in the South. Carpenters would buy lumber from a mill that had been machined, but they would then work on projects entirely with hand tools from that point forward. If a particular utility project like a bench used a component where the original edge is intact as it was cut at the mill, it might still bear milling marks from the machinery. Therefore, circular saw or bandsaw marks would be appropriate. (Assuming, of course, that the carpenter did not use a hand plane, scraper or sandpaper to remove the marks.) These marks would exist only on the edges and surfaces of the larger boards, however, and not on smaller pieces the carpenter cut himself. Those pieces would almost exclusively show marks made by a common handsaw.

*Bandsaw marks are similar in appearance to those made by mechanized or foot-powered scrollsaws of the period.*

*With the wood darkened with mineral spirits, you can see the series of fine planer marks on this piece of walnut.*

If boards had been surfaced with a mechanical planer at the mill, which was fairly common, they might bear the milling marks on the surface. These are usually faint washboard-like marks that result from where the multiple knives of the planer cutterhead contacted the surface as the cutterhead rotated. Modern boards from your local home center, however, have a much finer pattern of milling marks than would have existed in the 1860s. Likewise, any milling marks made by a typical shop planer would also be smaller. For authenticity, these milling marks should be removed from all wood surfaces in your reproduction project. A cabinet scraper or sandpaper will work fine for this.

Let's take a closer look at some of the markings you're likely to make in your own shop.

**Bandsaw**—Bandsaw marks are generally vertical lines on board edges, and nearly always perpendicular to the face. An electric jigsaw makes the same marks, although a bit more coarsely. An 1860s craftsman wouldn't have had a bandsaw or jigsaw, but he very well may have had a foot-powered scrollsaw that would make the same

marks. A handheld coping saw, fretsaw or even a regular handsaw could also make the same vertical marks. Any markings of this type on your project would not be inauthentic to the period.

**Circular saw**—Circular saw marks are curved lines on board faces or edges. Although these would have been common on milled lumber of the period, the blades used in mills were huge, so the curved lines would have a very large radius making for a very gentle curve. The marks made by modern-shop circular saws have a much smaller radius, making for tight, very obvious curves. These marks are not period-correct and should be removed wherever they appear.

**Planer**—As discussed earlier, the milling marks of modern planers are not period-correct and should be removed. Be especially aware that lumber fresh from your local home center will likely have these marks.

**Router**—Routers can make a distinguishable marking similar to that made by a planer, but on a much smaller area and almost always on board edges. These marks are not period-correct and should be removed wherever visible. For the projects in this book, you might use a router only for making tenons, rabbets and grooves, so any marks made will be hidden inside joints. No need to remove them.

**Sanders**—Sandpaper was common in the 1860s (it was patented in the U.S. in 1834), but it was always used by hand and thus left no distinctive machine-like markings. Modern sanding machines can leave a couple types of distinct markings. Disk sanders, handy for smoothing flat and convex curved edges, can leave a very distinct and visible series of fine curved lines on a workpiece edge. These are not period-correct and should be removed wherever visible.

Handheld power sanders are great for smoothing large, flat surfaces quickly, but they can also leave a unique marking of tiny swirls in the wood surface. These swirls are often invisible until a finish coating is applied to the wood, such as stain or an oil finish, at which point they pop out. Both unsightly and inauthentic to the period, they should be removed. When using a power sander, always gradually move to the next finer grit of sandpaper, which will help remove the swirls. It's a good idea to always follow up power sanding by hand sanding in the direction of the grain to remove any swirls that may have been created.

## RIVETING

I stated earlier that this book isn't a tutorial. However, there are two techniques you'll need to use that aren't commonly covered in woodworking books. Rivets were frequently used in the 19th century for any type of item that required two pieces of wood to pivot against each other. Three projects in this book use rivets, so let's take a look at what you need to know, as well as a few alternatives.

As with most fasteners of the period, rivets were made of iron, mild steel, brass and copper. Specialized riveting tools are available today, but because the metal is fairly soft, riveting is easily accomplished with standard shop tools.

*Disk sanders can leave a distinctive series of curved lines on board edges.*

*Swirl marks from an electric sander, sometimes called pigtails because of their spiral nature, are never period-correct for 19th-century work.*

Step 1

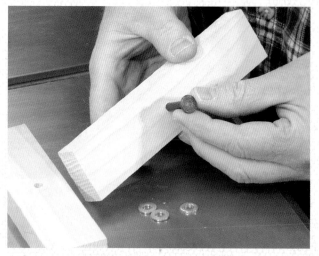

Step 2

Step 3

**1)** For each riveted joint, you'll need a rivet and a pair of washers of the appropriate size. You'll also need a ball-peen hammer (although a regular hammer will do in a pinch), a good pair of side cutters, and a solid surface on which to work. A steel anvil is best, but a concrete floor or block will do. For photography purposes, I did this rivet on the cast iron top of my tablesaw, but I wouldn't recommend that for regular use.

**2)** Start by drilling a hole sized to match the rivet through both workpieces. Here, the hole is ¼" to accept the size rivet used in the Camp Stool and Lt. Kelly's Camp Chair projects. Check that the rivet slides smoothly into the hole without either binding or having too much play. It's wise to first drill a hole in a piece of scrap to perform this test before drilling the actual workpiece.

**3)** With the rivet inserted into the first workpiece, slip on a rivet washer. This will create a small gap between the two workpieces, allowing them to pivot smoothly without rubbing against each other.

**4)** Slip the second workpiece over the rivet and top with another washer. Using the side cutters (or a powered grinder), trim the rivet so it stands about half its diameter above the washer. For this ¼" rivet, I cut it so ⅛" protrudes above the washer.

Step 4

Step 5

Step 6

Step 7

**5)** Strike the protruding end of the rivet squarely once or twice with the flat side of the ball peen hammer. This will flatten the rivet a bit, and at this point the tip of the rivet is slightly wider than the washer opening.

**6)** Still using the flat of the hammer, strike the rivet at a slight angle around all edges. As shown in the photo, the rivet will begin to take on a mushroom-like shape.

**7)** Switch to the rounded side of the hammer and continue striking the rivet around the edges, further expanding it. Work slowly and aim carefully, taking care not to hit the wood.

**8)** Continue the process until the tip of the rivet assumes a rounded shape that has expanded snugly against the washer.

If you're willing to compromise a bit, there are two other types of rivets that, while not period-correct, are not obviously so. The first is a hollow rivet, sometimes called a hollow-core rivet. This type of rivet existed in the 19th century, but was uncommon except in larger industrial cities. It would never have been used on items made in the field. As the name implies, the tip of the rivet is not solid. To attach a hollow rivet, either a specialized crimping tool or a short metal rod with a cone-shaped tip is pressed into the hollow tip. Struck with a hammer, the hollow tip quickly begins to

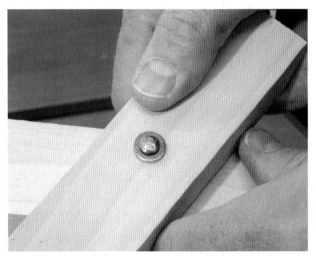

Step 8

*Hollow rivets (shown in sequence in the piece of wood) are flattened with a hammer and crimping tool. Below the wood are two-piece rivets, which slip into either side of the drilled holes and snap together with the sharp tap of a hammer.*

flower out. Once the hollow rim is sufficiently expanded, a few taps with a hammer will flatten it to the workpiece. This type of rivet is commonly used without a washer. While the hollow side of the rivet is easy to distinguish, the rivet head looks exactly like a standard rivet.

The other type of rivet is a two piece arrangement, shown just below the hollow rivets in the above photo. A hollow rivet is slipped into the hole in one workpiece, while a matching solid rivet is slipped through a hole in the other. A tap with a hammer snaps the two pieces together internally. This rivet did not exist in the 1860s, but since each side of a joined pair looks identical to a standard flat-head rivet, it's difficult to identify as an anachronism. The choice is yours.

One type of rivet to avoid is the modern pop rivet, sometimes called a blind rivet. Not only are pop rivets usually made of aluminum, their design is strictly 20th century and not period-correct in appearance from any angle. Split rivets are period-correct as long as they're made of correct materials, but they aren't very strong and I don't recommend them for weight-bearing furniture.

## STENCILING

Two of the projects in this book require stenciled painting. I've included stencil templates for each project, which you can copy or scan, and print out at the appropriate size. The stencil for the Hardtack Crate project is larger than most printers can handle, so that one will have to be printed out in sections and taped together.

If you live in a larger metropolitan area, you may have a local sign maker or print shop that offers laser-cut stencils. Likewise, there are a number of companies online who offer this service. While all of these firms make custom stencils, because the laser cutters are computerized most can also make a stencil quite easily from a digital file. All that's needed is a high-resolution scanned digital image on disk, which they download to the cutter. They set the desired size for the finished stencil, then just hit a button and let the machine do its thing. A few minutes later, the stencil is done perfectly. Most offer stencils in a Mylar or other plastic material that will last for years, or more traditional heavy manila-like paper. Costs for this service vary widely, but it's usually in the range of $30 to $60 an hour. Some firms have a setup fee that may add to the cost. A simple stencil—say a two-line text stencil for the end of the Ammo Box project—might take anywhere from 15 minutes to a half-hour to produce, depending on the complexity and material used. A larger stencil like the one for the Hardtack Crate project will take longer and, consequently, will cost more.

You can, of course, cut your own stencils, but be forewarned that it is a very tedious process. It took me about five or six hours of steady work to cut out the stencil for the Hardtack Crate project.

Start by printing out the stencil templates included with the projects. You can do this with an enlarging photocopy machine (your local office supply store will have one), or scanning the templates into your computer and then printing it out at the appropriate size. Once you have your printout, cover it with a peel-off clear plastic laminate. This will both strengthen the paper for cutting and make it last longer in use. Smooth the laminate down securely. Slip a cutting mat (or thick cardboard or other sacrificial material) under the printout and carefully, slowly cut out each letter with a sharp utility knife. As you work, replace the blade frequently so you always have the sharpest edge possible; my knife has break-off tips that make the process quick. Be especially careful when cutting the tiny connectors on the individual letters, as they can tear easily. Also, be mindful of where you rest your hands, as it's easy to tear out the connectors on letters you've already cut. If you should accidentally tear or break one of the letter connectors, cover the letter with Scotch tape and re-cut it.

Attach the stencil to your project with masking tape around the edges, carefully pulling it taut. Because your stencil is thin paper, it may tend to curl at points, especially at curves in letters, so use pins to hold the stencil flat to the surface where needed. A paint brush with short, stiff bristles

works best for painting stencils (it's what they used back then, too), but a foam brush may offer you more control. Dip the brush into the paint but don't thoroughly soak it. Then brush off most of the paint on a piece of scrap wood or paper; the idea is that you want the brush to be almost dry, but still have enough paint to coat the exposed surfaces in the cutouts. Use a brush with too much paint on it and you'll have paint running underneath the stencil. That's not inauthentic, however, and a lot of surviving stenciled ammo boxes have some rushed-looking paint jobs. A little leak-through around the edges is perfectly period-correct, but you don't want to overdo it.

Go over the entire stencil, applying the paint in a dabbing motion. Be sure the stencil doesn't move during painting. Let it dry a bit—just enough that the paint is no longer liquid—then remove the tape and pins and peel back the stencil. Don't let the paint dry completely, or the stencil will adhere to your project and you'll have to tear it off in pieces.

*Cutting stencils by hand is slow, careful work.*

*Dabbing with a nearly dry paintbrush is the best way to create crisp, attractive lettering with a stencil.*

Hide glue comes in dry form, and is mixed with water and heated before use.

Although it has the same properties as traditionally prepared glue, liquid hide glue is far easier to use.

## GLUE

Today's woodworker has a huge variety of adhesives from which to choose, but during the mid-19th century hide glue was king. This glue was made from the collagen found in animal hides, which is where jokes about taking old, nag horses to the "glue factory" came from. Hide glue is readily available today and comes in packages that contain dry, amber-colored nuggets or granules that must be mixed with water and heated to around 140–150 degrees before use. There are specialized heaters available for this, but it can also be prepared in a home-made double boiler. Once properly prepared, hide glue is brushed onto a woodworking joint, which is then clamped tightly. The glue cools and hardens quickly, and makes for a strong joint.

The process of preparing and using hide glue can be a messy one, and the glue itself can be difficult to use since it must remain at the right temperature and consistency throughout the application process. It's particularly problematic to apply to large areas as it begins to cure rapidly, often before you've managed to get the glue on the entire workpiece. To put it bluntly, hide glue can be a pain to use. Fortunately, a liquid version is available today that has urea added to the formula to keep it in liquid form. Urea was not unknown in the 1860s (it was discovered in the late 1700s),

but liquid hide glue simply wasn't used during the period. The working properties are about the same as the traditional heated type, so it doesn't greatly impact authenticity. Still, it can be finicky if you're not used to using it.

For complete authenticity for your Civil War reproductions, only traditional hide glue should be used. However, this is one area where I am more than willing to make a compromise. For almost all projects in this book that require glue, I've used standard, modern shop glue and I'm comfortable with that compromise. You, of course, may choose to do otherwise.

## Construction variations

One of the most important things to keep in mind when making the reproductions in this book is that there were few standards regarding sizes and construction methods. For some items like the Ammo Box and Hardtack Crate projects, there were actual U.S. and C.S. Army specifications in place for their size and construction. Suppliers, however, often ignored the specs, especially later in the war. For common items for which there were no official specs, there simply were no standards since mass production on a nationwide scale did not yet exist in the U.S. (or anywhere else). All the mass-produced stools that came from a furniture company on one side of Chicago often bore little resemblance to mass-produced stools for a company on the other side of town.

For that matter, even the Army-specified dimensions were vague. The regulations called for the exact size of an ammo box for musket cartridges, for example, but nowhere in the regulations is it mentioned what thickness or kind of wood to use. As a result, there was a huge variation in woodworking items even among those ordered by the military. For things made by small-town carpenters, and especially by soldiers in the field, the variety of sizes and styles was even greater.

What this means is that you should feel free to alter the dimensions and construction details of the projects in this book. I'd try to stick closely to military specs on the two projects that include them, but alter all the others just about any way you wish in a period-appropriate manner. I'll make suggestions in this regard where appropriate for each of the projects.

## Finishing

There is a wide variety of finish coatings available today, many of which can greatly protect furniture from the elements. Very few of these are period-correct, but those that are remain very close to what was used then.

For clear coating, there were three main choices: a drying oil, shellac and wax. That's about it. Oil-based varnishes existed, but were rarely used because fast-drying shellac did the same job far more easily and effectively. A drying oil such as boiled linseed oil could be rubbed to a moderate sheen, and repeated applications offered a small amount of protection. Rubbed oil finishes do not impart a lot of protection from water, however, so a rubbed oil finish was often topped with a coat of wax that was replenished regularly.

For greater protection and a higher-gloss appearance, shellac was the number one choice. Easy to make and easy to apply, shellac is still readily available today in both dry and liquid form. Making shellac from scratch (by adding denatured alcohol to the dry shellac granules or flakes) is more authentic to the period, as liquid shellac has a very short shelf life and was rarely kept on hand. The formulation of today's liquid shellac isn't quite the same as making it yourself, as well. However, the finished results of either type are indistinguishable. Shellac gave pretty good protection and a nice gloss to furniture of the day.

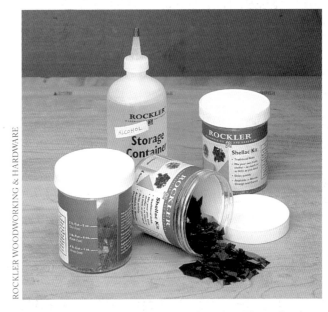

*Shellac, either as a commercially prepared liquid or in dry form as shown here, is one of the oldest protective clear-coat finishes for furniture.*

*Boiled linseed oil brings out the inner beauty in this piece of cherry.*

I favor boiled linseed oil—usually known to woodworkers simply as BLO—for projects made with hardwoods such as walnut, cherry, oak and maple. The oil darkens the wood nicely, and brings out the grain of woods like cherry. A few applications give as much protection as I need, and beautifies whatever it touches. Be aware that the BLO you'll buy today isn't the same formulation as what they used back then (the original had lead in it, for one thing), but the final results are identical. It is possible to make your own, but the process involves a lot more than just tossing some raw oil in a pot and throwing it on the stove. In fact, the process can be quite dangerous and I do not recommend it. Making the compromise of using modern BLO is one I strongly suggest for Civil War reproductions; it's more than authentic enough.

Paint was used then just as now, and for all the same reasons. Paints today are far different from those of the period, of course, but this is another area where a small compromise is a safer way to go. Mixing up your own paint is possible (the ordnance manuals for both armies list the exact "recipes" for several paints in Chapter Seven of the manuals), but

I strongly recommend against it. Finding some of the listed ingredients—such as litharge, copperas, pulverized Spanish whiting and turkey umber—will be difficult at best, and potentially dangerous. Litharge, for example, is lead oxide. Again, this is an area where compromising by using the modern equivalent is the sensible way to go.

When choosing paint, for authenticity avoid latex and stick with oil-based formulations. Paints of the period did not have as high a sheen as today's high-gloss paints, so a semi-gloss paint is a better choice. (Generally speaking, the more pigment a period paint had, the less gloss it had.) In use, most oil-based paints of the period quickly dulled to a satin or even flat appearance.

Two other types of paints that are period-correct are milk paint and whitewash. Both were common throughout the 19th century. Neither is particularly durable, although whitewash does lend a bit of protection and beauty to exterior wooden structures. (It has an annoying tendency to rub off onto skin and clothing when leaned against, however, so it's not suitable for furniture.)

The final finishing method is not only easy, but it's the only one that guarantees a 100% period-correct appearance: none at all. Carpenters of the time usually applied oil, shellac or paint only to furniture that was to be used indoors, and not always to that. Furniture and other items that were to be used outdoors would have been finished with paint only or maybe BLO, or not coated in any way. An item made in the field by a soldier might have been painted, but more likely it was left raw.

## One final note...

In the photos that accompany each project, I've removed guards for photographic reasons to make each procedure easier to see. However, I urge you to use all appropriate guards and safety practices when using power tools.

*Part Two*

# THE PROJECTS

*Members of the Union brigade of the National Civil War Association.*

# Chapter 3:
# FIVE-BOARD BENCH

"An army marches on its stomach" is an oft-quoted phrase credited to Napoleon Bonaparte. And while that observation is certainly true, any soldier will tell you that an army sits on another part of the anatomy.

This bench is about as basic a piece of furniture as you can imagine, and its roots go back much further than the Civil War. Soldiers and citizens during the American Revolution used these benches (I can imagine a sign on one boasting, "Washington sat here"), as did the people of Europe and other nations. With only five components—and two of them come in identical pairs—it is quick to build, yet extremely sturdy. Among the easiest projects in this book, the bench features only straight cuts, very basic joinery, and needs just a handful of nails for fasteners.

I promised that a number of the projects in this book would utilize standard ¾" lumber, so I've made this bench using a piece of off-the-shelf 1x12 white pine from the local home center. You can use any wood species, of course, but keep in mind regional differences—a Confederate bench would more likely be made of yellow pine. Many of these benches were made in the field during the Civil War, so would most likely have been constructed with SPF lumber, but feel free to use any hardwood. Thicker lumber will work fine (standard 2-by construction lumber would make for

*Clerks at the headquarters of the assistant adjutant general relax on a pair of common five-board benches.*

## *Cut List*

## FIVE-BOARD BENCH

Overall Dimensions: 11" x 18¾" x 36"

| Name | Qty. | Wood | Dimensions |
|---|---|---|---|
| Seat/Top | 1 | SPF | ¾" x 11" x 36" |
| Sides | 2 | SPF | ¾" x 3½" x 36" |
| Legs | 2 | SPF | ¾" x 11" x 18" |

*See drawing on page 33*

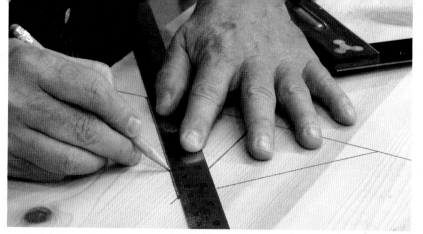

*Figure 1*

*Figure 2*

a heavy, very sturdy bench), but for strength issues don't use anything thinner than ¾". You can also mix wood thicknesses, say ¾" for the seat and side pieces, and 2-by stock for the legs; a mixing of lumber would be quite authentic.

## Stock preparation

Begin by cutting all the components to width. Obviously, the two side pieces and the two leg supports are identical, so you'll have your components ready to go in quick order. Because I didn't want this bench to be the exact width of off-the-shelf lumber, something that's extremely over-represented in the hobby, I trimmed my 1x12 (which is only 11¼" wide, remember) to 11".

The bottoms of the leg supports have a triangular cutout in the middle, effectively turning a single, wide foot into two, which will allow the bench to set more evenly on the ground. This triangular shape can be any size you want (for that matter, it can be circular instead of triangular), but try to make each of the feet created by the cutout at least 2" wide.

Essentially what I did was to first pencil in a centerline at the bottom of the leg support, making a mark at 5". I then marked the bottom of the support 2" in from each side, and drew lines from these marks to my 5" mark on the centerline to create the triangle shape as in Fig. 1. Because the two leg supports were the same, I didn't cut them to

length yet, but instead laid them out mirror image to each other and marked the triangle cuts for both at the same time.

Cut the leg supports to length and cut out the triangle (Fig. 2). I used the bandsaw for this, but a scrollsaw, jigsaw or handsaw work just as well for these simple cuts.

Although it isn't necessary, you'll find that the bench is a lot sturdier if the side pieces are inset into cutout notches at the upper portion of the leg supports. This cutout must be sized exactly to the side pieces for a snug fit, but that's easy to do. When you cut the side pieces to length, first cut off a small piece about ¾" to 1" thick to act as a guide. Just lay this guide at the top of the leg support and trace around it (Fig. 3), then cut out the notches.

Finally, cut the corners off the bottoms of the side pieces to remove what would otherwise be sharp corners. The size of this angled cut is

*Figure 3*

Figure 4

Figure 5

unimportant, but I measured the corners and made marks at 1½" and 2½", then drew a line between the marks to create the cutline. These corners can also be rounded instead of straight.

## Assembly

On a flat surface, set the two sidepieces upright parallel to each other and nail the seat in place atop them. Box nails or fine-finish nails from 2½" to 3" in length work well for this task, and four or five nails down each side of the seat will do the trick to create the seat assembly. Using a nail set, drive all of the nails so they're just below the surface of the wood. This will prevent nail heads from snagging on clothing.

Mark a pencil line 4" from the ends on the top and sides of the seat assembly; this will be your nail line for the leg supports. Lay the seat assembly on its side and slip the leg supports into place such they are centered on your nail line. The leg supports should fit snugly into the notches on either side.

Drive a single nail through the lower portion of the side piece and into each leg support, then flip it over and do the same on the other side.

Turn the bench upright on a firm surface (the floor is best) but keep in mind that at this point the leg supports are not firmly fixed, so don't put all your weight on it—with a single nail on each side, the leg supports will pivot. Adjust one leg support so it's perfectly square to the seat assembly, and drive a pair of nails through the seat and into the top of the leg support as in Fig. 4, then repeat with the other side.

The legs are now firm, but we still need to add a couple more nails. Lay the bench on its side once again and drive a nail through the upper edge of the side piece and into the top of the leg supports on all four sides (Fig. 5).

Set the completed bench on a flat surface and check to see that it sits level. If not, use some coarse sandpaper wrapped around a wood block to slightly trim the underside of the long foot. This is only necessary if the bench will be used on a flat surface, of course; if you intend to take this bench out to reenactments or Living History encampments, chances are that you'll never find a level spot to set it down anyway.

At this point your bench is complete. It's perfectly period-correct to leave the wood raw and allow the wood to weather naturally, and if your goal is to re-create a bench that might have been made in the field it's best to leave it unfinished. If you do decide to add a finish, an oil-based paint is your best choice for exterior use.

## Variations

Because it is so basic, the five-board bench is among the most modifiable projects in this book. To begin with, all the dimensions can be altered to match your seating needs or even available materials. Made according to these instructions, no changes are necessary for a bench up to 4' or 5' in length.

For a longer bench, consider adding a third leg support in the center.

If you make the leg supports a bit taller and shorten both the top and sides, the five-board bench can be altered to serve as a small table, as shown in the historical example in Fig. 6. Shorten the leg supports in addition to the seat assembly, and you've got a five-board stepstool.

If you don't want to create those notches in the legs to inset the side pieces, alter the construction as follows: Cut the components to length and width as before, omitting the step of cutting the notches. Don't cut the bottom triangles in the leg supports yet. Nail the seat to the side pieces as before, and then measure the exact distance between the side pieces from the underside of the seat assembly. (If you use ¾" stock, the distance should be 9½".) Trim the width of the leg supports to this measurement so the legs will fit between the sidepieces. Now mark and cut your bottom triangles into the leg supports, then nail them in place as before. While a bench constructed this way is also period-correct,

keep in mind that making the bench without the inset cutouts for the leg supports will result in a bench that is a bit less sturdy. Those cutouts acts as rabbet joints, adding structural support. Plus, to make those leg supports fit between the side pieces, they are now narrower than before.

Speaking of those triangles, as mentioned earlier, they don't have to be triangular at all. The cutout can be a curve instead.

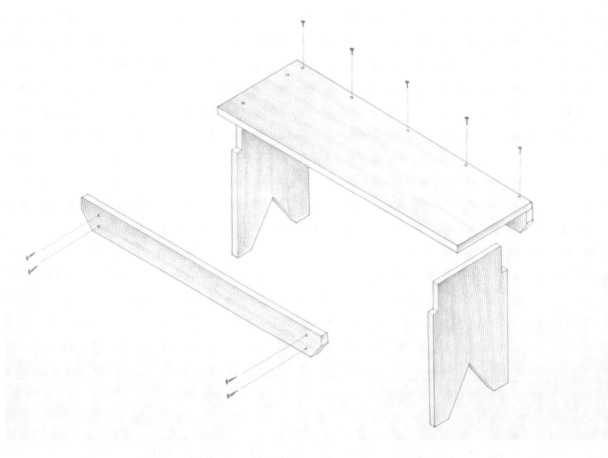

**50 lbs.**     **Nett.**

# ARMY BREAD
### FROM
## ROBERT STEARS
## 93 BOERUM ST
### ◄·►
### BROOKLYN
## U.S.
## SUBDEP

*Sep.t*

*1862*

*Captain J.W. Forsyth, Provost Marshal, poses with a shipment of hardtack at Aquia Creek, Va., in 1863.*

# Chapter 4:
# HARDTACK CRATE

The soldiers of both the North and the South hated it, but they ate literally tons of it. They called it things like "worm castles," "bullet stoppers," and "teeth dullers." Hardtack, a simple, impossibly hard cracker made from only three ingredients (and sometimes only two) was a staple of the soldier's diet.

The hardtack crate is one of only two projects in this book that had specific requirements from the U.S. Army regarding construction. (The Confederate regulations don't mention hardtack crates.) The earliest recorded specs came from Lt. Col. C.L. Kilburn, the Assistant Commissary General of Subsistence. In 1863 in his *Notes on Preparing Stores for the United States Army*. Kilburn wrote that, "The packages should be thoroughly seasoned, (of wood imparting no taste or odor to the bread,) and reasonably tight. The usual method now adopted is to pack 50 pounds net, in basswood boxes, (sides, top and bottom ½ inch, ends ⅝ of an inch,) and of dimensions corresponding with the cutters used, and strapped at each end with light iron or wood."

*Clerks of the Commissary Dept. supervise the unloading of a trainload of hardtack at Aquia Creek, Va.*

## *Cut List*

## HARDTACK CRATE

**Overall Dimensions: 11" x 17" x 26"**

| Name | Qty. | Wood | Dimensions |
|------|------|------|------------|
| Sides | 2 | SPF | ⅝" x 9¾" x 26" |
| Ends | 2 | SPF | 1" x 9¾" x 15¾" |
| Top/Bottom | 2 | SPF | ⅝" x 17" x 26" (a) |
| Lid Cleats | 2 | SPF | 1" x 1" x 15¾" (b) |

**Notes:**

(a) Top/Bottom dimensions are finished size and do not include tongue.

(b) Inside width of crate is 15¾", so cleat should be just slightly shorter.

*See drawing on page 45*

In 1864, August V. Kautz, in his *Customs Of Service For Non-Commissioned Officers And Soldiers*, gave a more expanded description of a hardtack crate's construction. "When hard bread is put in boxes (the best packages for field transportation), they should be made of fully-seasoned wood, of a kind to impart no taste or odor to the bread, and as far as practicable of single pieces. When two pieces are used in making the same surface, they should be tongued and grooved together. A box 26x17x11 inches, exterior measure, is an average box for pilot bread, under the usual circumstances of land transportation. The ends of a box of this size should be made of inch, and the remainder of five-eighths, stuff, the package well strapped with green hickory or other suitable wood."

As you can see, even though Kilburn notes that basswood was usually used, neither set of guidelines definitively requires a particular wood species, and Kilburn's description neglects to state the overall dimensions of the crate. Further, in spite of the guidelines from both officers, individual contractors frequently ignored the recommendations. (The same was true for ammo boxes, as I'll discuss in the next chapter.) Surviving samples of hardtack crates sometimes used lapped joints instead of tongue-and-groove to create wider panels, for example, and stock thicknesses were all over the board.

## Stock preparation

Because his dimensions are more complete, I've elected to make the Kautz hardtack crate here. Also, part of my goal here is to help you create long-lasting reproductions, and the thicker dimensions of the Kautz crate lend themselves well to a crate that, although a bit heavier than the Kilburn crate, will withstand years of use. The Kautz crate, because it uses no stock that is ¾" thick, helps combat the over-representation of wooden items in that thickness.

The Kautz crate uses 1" and ⅝" stock, so you'll first need to acquire or create lumber of those thicknesses. If you have a lumber supplier in your area, you may be able to have a quantity of stock prepared for you in these thicknesses, although it will be more expensive than doing it yourself. For the thicker end pieces, a standard 2x12 pine board

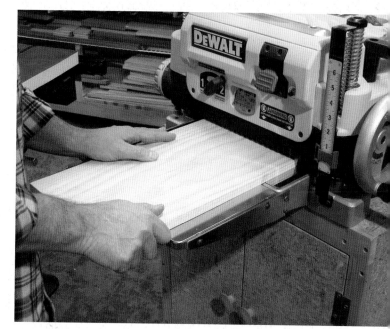

*Figure 1*

works fine when planed to 1" for the crate ends, per Kautz. For all other stock, you can plane ¾" lumber to ⅝". (Fig. 1) It's always best to plane the lumber to thickness before cutting the components to final size.

If the milling process has left planer marks, remove them now; it'll be easier than doing it after it's been cut. A sanding block with a coarse paper—say 80-grit or lower—will take care of this quickly without making the lumber too smooth. Cut the two ends and two sides to size (we'll get to the top and bottom shortly).

# MAKING YOUR OWN HARDTACK

Hardtack is easy to make, and the ingredients couldn't be simpler. But good luck finding an exact, government-specified recipe.

Generally, hardtack was made with flour, water and salt, but exact proportions (and whether salt was used and how much) depended on the contractor making it, so there were really quite a few "authentic" hardtack recipes. The size of the hardtack cracker also varied ridiculously—there are Library of Congress photos that show hardtack in the more commonly recognized size of about 3" x 3" inches, but also a few photos of soldiers holding crackers the size of dinner plates. Square hardtack was the norm, but there are photos of round crackers, too.

The flour used then was a specific cracker flour. You can get by with regular, unbleached flour, but a half-and-half mix of all-purpose and pastry flour is a fair approximation.

No matter what recipe I cite here, I'm sure I can start an argument among those with differing opinions as to its authenticity. However, the following recipe should serve you well. Adjust the amounts as you please depending on the size of the batch you want to make, but hardtack proportions were generally:

1 cup flour
1 tsp salt (or less)
½ cup (or less) water

For best results, dissolve the salt in the water before adding water to the flour. In a large bowl, add just enough water to the flour to make a firm, stiff dough. If the dough is sticky, you've added too much water; if it falls apart, you've not added quite enough. Knead the dough thoroughly.

Roll out the dough between ⅜" and ½". Cut into squares about 3" x 3"; a dedicated hardtack cutter is great for this, put a pizza cutter works quite well. Use a thin dowel or a barbecue skewer to poke a 4-by-4 or staggered pattern of holes into the cracker. Place crackers on an ungreased cookie sheet.

Bake in a 375 degree oven for 25-30 minutes, flip the crackers, and bake for another 25-30 minutes. (These times are very approximate, depending on cracker thickness and final water content. Consider the crackers done when they turn a light brown.)

Remove crackers from oven and allow to thoroughly air-dry for a day or two. If there is any water content left in the crackers before storage, they will get moldy. Well-baked, completely dry hardtack can be stored almost indefinitely if kept dry.

# Crate assembly

Do a dry assembly of the crate on a flat surface to check for fit of all four components, as in Fig. 2. A dry assembly generally describes assembling a project without glue, but is always a good practice for any woodworking project, whether glue is used or not.

Start the assembly by attaching a side piece to two of the end pieces. Decide at this point whether you want to use glue. Hardtack crates were highly disposable and only had to stay together long enough to arrive at their destination in one piece, so glue wasn't used in their construction (or for any other shipping crates of the period, for that matter).

Figure 2

I recommend glue be used on the four corner joints if you plan to use your crate for a long time.

Place the two end pieces on end, apply glue to the end surfaces, then top with one of the side pieces. Unlike modern wire nails, because the tips of cut nails are square they rarely cause splitting. However, the nails in the corner joints are only ½" from the ends of the sides, so I recommend drilling a pilot hole before nailing. I used four 2½" nails at each corner of the crate for strength, but 2" nails are

fine, especially if the corner joints are glued. (Fig. 3) Although a carpenter of the period may or may not have set the nails after construction—the practice varied widely—driving the nails just below the surface with a nail set is a good idea.

Check the partial assembly for square, then repeat the nailing process with the other side piece. If using glue, allow the assembly to dry.

Figure 3

# Panel construction

The top and bottom of the Kautz crate measure 17" wide, so you'll need to mate two separate pieces to create them. Per Kautz, we'll use a tongue-and-groove joint, the most common means at the time of joining wood for this purpose.

Get an exact measure of the length by laying the complete crate frame on top of a pair of ⅝" boards and marking them to length as in Fig. 4. Why not just cut these pieces to length at the same time you cut the side pieces, since they're the same length? I did it this way for two reasons. By

Figure 4

making the crate frame first and then matching the top and bottom to it, you can compensate for any slight errors in making the crate frame. If it ended up being slightly long or short, the boards will now match exactly. Also, in the event that your crate frame isn't quite square, you can mark these boards to match the crate, thereby compensating for any slight deviation of squareness. Mark the two boards you'll use for the bottom, then flip the crate over and mark the two for the top. Be sure to label each board so you use them in the correct order and orientation.

Cut the boards for the bottom and top to length, but not yet to width, as creating the tongue-and-groove joint will subtract a bit of width from one of each pair of boards. Speaking of width, I should mention at this point that it's not necessary at all for the two components making up these panels to be the same size. I made mine from the same length of board just as you probably will, so mine were the same width, but you could just as easily cut one component from a 7"-wide board and the other from a 10" board. It doesn't matter at all if the joint isn't in the center of the panel; what matters is that the final panel be a total of 17" wide.

Tongue-and-groove joints can be cut in various ways—by hand with planes, on a router table, and on the tablesaw, with the latter method being the easiest. (For all that follows, I'll assume that your saw has a standard ⅛"-thick blade. If you use a thin-kerf blade, adjust accordingly.)

For joints of this type—mortise-and-tenon joints are based on the same principle—it's best to make the groove first, then fine-tune whatever goes into it to the correct size. The general rule for sizing for these joints is to make the tongue or tenon about ⅓ the thickness of the workpiece. We could make that exact, but for stock that's ⅝" thick, a third of that would be ³⁄₂₄", a truly odd dimension that would be difficult to measure. This is a case where close enough is not only easier, but also more authentic—you can bet that for utility items like shipping crates they weren't that fussy back then.

Using one of the ⅝"-thick boards as a guide, set your tablesaw's fence so that the blade falls about in the center of the board edge—again, it doesn't have to be exact. Lock down the fence, and raise the blade to ¼" high. Pass the board over the blade to make a groove in the board's edge. (Fig. 5) Now, flip the board end-for-end so that the other face is against the fence and make the pass again on the same edge. This makes two cuts, each the exact

Figure 5

# SINGING FOR SUPPER

In 1854, Stephen Foster wrote the melancholy, but popular, "Hard Times Come Again No More." The song itself was popular among soldiers of both sides during the conflict, but a wartime parody that substituted a certain reviled cracker became just as popular in both the North and South. There are a number of variations, but this set of lyrics is typical.

Let us close our game of poker, take our
tin cups in our hand
As we all stand by the cook-tent door.
As dried mummies of hard crackers, are
handed to each man.
O, hardtack, come again no more!

*Chorus:*
*'Tis the song, the sigh of the hungry:*
*"Hardtack, hardtack, come again no more."*
*Many days you have lingered upon our*
*stomachs sore.*
*O, hardtack, come again no more!*

'Tis a hungry, thirsty soldier who
wears his life away
In torn clothes—his better days are o'er.
And he's sighing now for whiskey in a voice
as dry as hay,
"O, hardtack, come again no more!"

*Chorus*

'Tis the wail that is heard in camp
both night and day,
'Tis the murmur that's mingled
with each snore.
'Tis the sighing of the soul for
spring chickens far away,
"O, hardtack, come again no more!"

*Chorus*

But to all these cries and murmurs,
there comes a sudden hush
As frail forms are fainting by the door.
For they feed us now on horse feed that
the cooks call mush!
O, hardtack, come again once more!

*Final Chorus:*
*'Tis the dying wail of the starving:*
*"O, hardtack, hardtack, come again once more!"*
*You were old and very wormy, but we*
*pass your failings o'er.*
*O, hardtack, come again once more!*

---

same distance from the fence, so the groove is now perfectly centered. Eyeball the resulting groove, and if it's approximately ⅓ as wide as the board, you're done. If it's too narrow, nudge the fence a hair closer to the blade, lock it down, and do the double-pass again with the same board. Once you're satisfied with the groove in this first piece, leave the fence where it is and cut the other board.

You now have two boards—one from the crate top and one from the bottom—with grooves. To create the matching tongues, first move the tablesaw fence out of the way. Lay one of the boards with the grooved edge against the saw blade, then adjust the blade height so the tips of the teeth come just to the edge of the groove. Lock the blade and attach a sacrificial face to the fence; a long piece of scrap is fine. Adjust the fence so that it just barely kisses the blade and lock it down. Run the edge of the first mating board over the blade on one side, then flip the board and do the other, as in Fig. 6. Check the tongue to be sure it fits the groove, then make the same cuts in the other board. You now have a tongue on both boards, but it's only about ⅛" long; our groove is ¼" deep, so we need to make another series

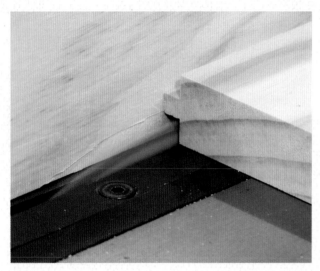

*Figure 6*

of cuts. Move the fence so that it is exactly ⅛" away from the blade and lock it down. Pass the boards over the blade as before. You now have tongues that are ¼" long.

Fit the two bottom pieces together *without glue* and place the crate frame on them as we did when determining the length, and mark for width. Take the bottom apart and trim the boards as necessary. Flip the crate frame upside down, reassemble the two boards for the bottom panel, and nail them in place.

I do not recommend gluing these two boards for the bottom panel together. Wood expands and contracts across its width in response to seasonal changes in humidity, and a solid panel of 17" would move sufficiently that it may split as it shrinks in less-humid conditions. By not gluing the two pieces making up these panels together, the individual 8½" boards making up the panel have room to move. (You'll probably notice that the gap at the tongue-and-groove joint gets a bit wider in the winter, and closes up in the summer. This is normal.) The amount wood moves depends on a variety of factors including wood species, grain direction, thickness, ambient air humidity and geography. It's quite possible that your 17" panel may not expand/contract enough to cause splitting if glued up, so feel free to give it a try for a sturdier crate. Just don't be surprised if a crack appears.

If you glued the corner joints of the crate frame, don't worry—because the grain of the sides and end pieces run in the same direction, they will expand/contract at the same rate at the corners. Splitting isn't an issue there.

## Topping it off

When shipping hardtack in the 1860s, the top of the crate would have been assembled without glue and nailed into place the same as the bottom. Crates were simply pried open in pieces, and the pieces most likely ended up in the campfire. However, your goal in building this crate is probably to use it as storage, and that means you'll want a lid that stays in one piece.

Make and assemble the top the same as you did the bottom, but add cleats to the underside of the top that will not only hold the two pieces of the top together, but also act as guides to keep the top in place. Cut two pieces of wood to a hair less than 15¾" (the same length as the end pieces). I cut some 1" strips from the same board I used for the crate ends, resulting in a pair of 1" x 1" cleats, but you can use cleats of any size. Cutting them just slightly less than 15¾" will ensure that the lid doesn't bind.

Locate the cleats 1" from each end of the underside of the top and centered between the side edges so that they will slip inside the crate when the lid is in place. Attach with four screws—two will end up in each of the boards making up the top, and the top panel can expand/contract freely at the center with the seasons. (Fig. 7) Measure carefully and use the correct length of screw so they don't end up sticking out the top.

Cleats were not used when constructing shipping crates of this type, so they are not period-correct. However, there are surviving samples of crates and boxes modified by soldiers that have cleats (as well as metal or leather hinges, handles, and other modifications), so adding cleats is not

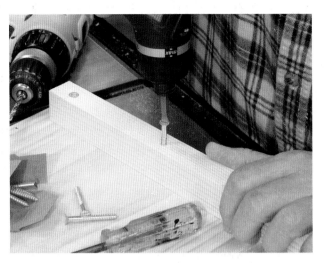

*Figure 7*

*Figure 8*

entirely inauthentic. If you are using your hardtack crate for storage of non-period items, the inside of the crate will not be seen anyway. Again, this is a compromise you'll need to consider.

With the lid finished, apply the stenciling (see the end of the chapter) as described in Chapter 2. The area of text in stencils for hardtack crates (and other crates) varied widely, so the final size of your stencil can vary. I patterned the stencil for the Robert Stears crate from a surviving example that appears in the book *Echoes of Glory: Arms and Equipment of the Union* and estimate the text area to be approximately 13" high by 17" long. The label for the A.T. Hanks crate is based on one on display at the Museum of Connecticut History in Hartford, Conn., and the text area for that stencil is approximately 10" x 13".

You can apply the stencil to just the top, or to both top and bottom; there are historical precedents for either way. In some cases, hardtack crates were also stenciled on the ends with the shipping destination, but this is also optional.

There are two final touches you'll want to consider for an authentic look. The first is to give the crate a just-opened look by adding nail holes to the lid—four along the

end edges, and four or five along the side edges. I did mine with a drill, then pressed nail heads into the holes to give them a correct squared appearance. If you really want it to look right, though, nail the lid on and then pry it off. They would have opened these crates with a hammer, axe or a combination of the two called a box tool, like the one in Fig. 8. A box tool was a tool of destruction, though, and the

*Lt. George T. Anthony of the 17th N.Y. battery (standing at left), poses with fellow officers in front of this tent. Note in the lower right of the photo that the officer has converted a hardtack crate into a camp chest.*

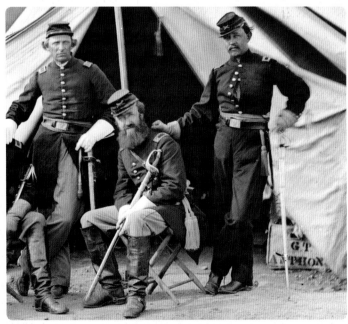

LIBRARY OF CONGRESS

results probably weren't pretty, so don't worry about being careful when you pry off the lid.

The final authentic touch is to add strapping to the crate. Metal straps were used during the period, but mostly for heavier crates; for hardtack crates, straps of green sapling were more common. Fibrous woods like hickory, ash or oak worked best, but saplings of any hardwood will work fine.

Take a hike through a nearby woods and collect some saplings about 6' tall and about ½" to ¾" thick. Split the sapling on the thicker end and if you're careful, you can pull it apart in two halves. You can also split the sapling with a drawknife, or use a hand plane to shave it down. The green sapling straps should bend easily around the corners of the crate (you can soak them in water for a few hours to make them more pliable). Start the sapling in the middle of one of the sides, attaching it with small nails or cut tacks. Continue wrapping the sapling around the crate ends, nailing it every four or five inches to hold it in place as in Fig. 9. Once all the way around the crate, overlap the ends and add one last nail or tack.

*Figure 9*

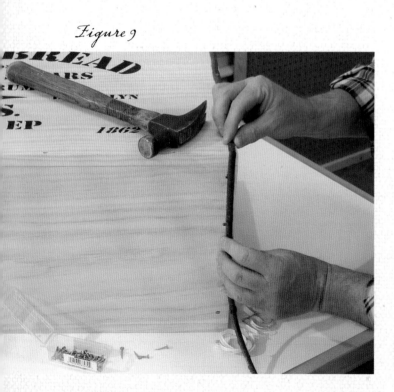

## Variations

Crates for shipping hardtack were designed to hold 50 lbs. of crackers. However, because different suppliers made hardtack crackers in various sizes, they varied the overall size of the crates as needed to accommodate packing 50 lbs. For that reason, you can alter the dimensions of your hardtack crate an inch or two in just about any direction.

If you intend to make your crate an obvious storage container—say, for example, you'd like to convert it to a period-style camp chest—you don't have to be secretive about adding cleats to the lid, as that would be an authentic soldier's modification. The same thing goes for adding wooden or metal handles to the crate ends, hinges and hasps to the lid edges, or even iron reinforcing brackets to the crate corners. (All of these modifications should be of period materials, of course.) For a camp chest, dividers can be added inside the crate; a lift-out tray can be added by attaching narrow support cleats to the inner crate walls.

For a thoroughly inauthentic modification, you can turn the crate into a cooler. Cut rigid foam insulation into rectangles sized to fit each interior surface. Attach these rectangles together to form a box-within-a-box arrangement; the foam can be joined with hot-melt glue or even duct tape. With this arrangement, the foam box acts as a sleeve that can be inserted into the crate, or removed as needed. Be sure the ends of the foam sleeve are low enough to accommodate the lid cleats, and don't forget to add a sheet of foam to the underside of the lid; a few dots of hot-melt glue will hold it in place. This foam sleeve isn't water-tight, of course, so don't be dumping a bag of ice in it or you'll have a leaky mess. However, those re-useable freezer packs work great.

Remember, however, that this last variation isn't even close to being period-correct, so don't ever let anyone see inside the crate.

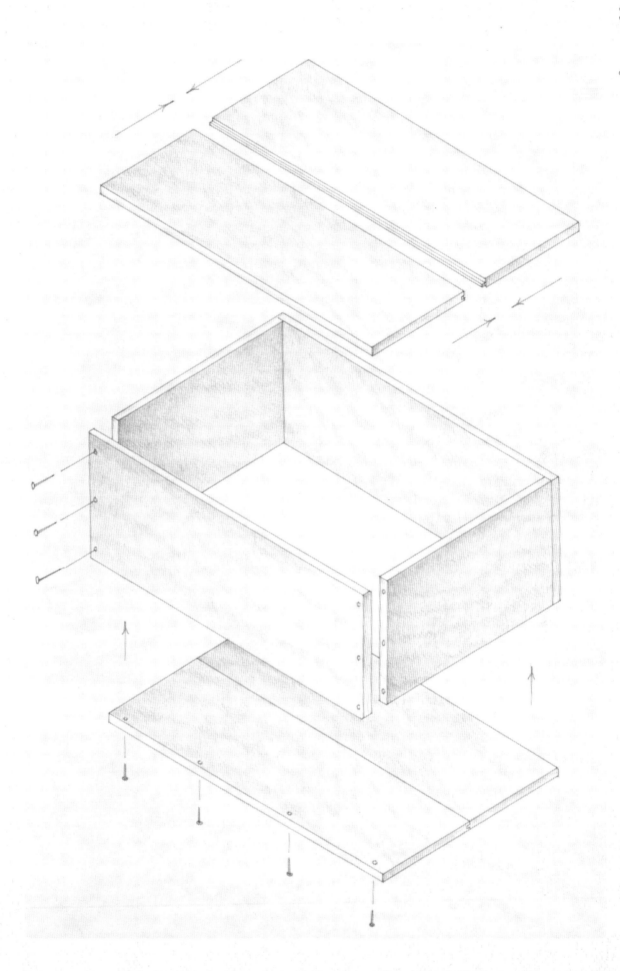

**ARMY BREAD**

50 lbs. Nett.

sept

1862

ROBERT STEARS

FROM

93 BOERUM St

BROOKLYN

U.S.

SUBDEP

*Use an enlarging copier or scan this stencil to create a printout of working size. Regardless of the overall size of the stencil, the text portion should measure approximately 13" high by 17".*

50 lbs    NET    ARMY BREAD    FROM    A. T. HANKS    70 & 72 Water St.    BROOKLYN    MAY    1862

*Use an enlarging copier or scan this stencil to create a printout of working size. Regardless of the overall size of the stencil, the text portion should measure approximately 8½" high by 13".*

*Ammunition Boxes, in Confederate works, Petersburg, Va., April 1865.*

# Chapter 5:
# AMMUNITION BOX

Like the hardtack crate in the previous chapter, boxes for shipping and storing ammunition had government specifications for size, material and construction. Also like hardtack crates, although there were some hard specs provided by the government, many specs were vague, leaving decisions for those up to the manufacturers.

The *Ordnance Manual for the Use of the Officers of the United States Army* states, "The boxes are made of white pine boards, dovetailed and nailed together, and are furnished with wooden brackets or handles nailed to the ends with wrought nails, clenched on the inside; the lids fastened with six 1.75 inch screws. They are painted different colors, to indicate the kind of cartridges. … Each box should be marked, on each end, with the number and kind of cartridges, and on the inside of the cover with the place and date of fabrication." The description and specs in the *Ordnance Manual for the Use of the Officers of the Confederate States Army* are identical, word-for-word.

For both armies, a chart was included in the manuals listing the interior box dimensions for each type of ammunition, which was an important difference from specs for hardtack crates. Because hardtack crackers came in a variety of sizes and thicknesses, the bakeries only needed to follow approximate dimensions for the crates—as long as the crate was about the right size, and as long as it could hold 50 pounds of crackers, it was fine. Ammunition cartridges, on the other hand, came in

*Ammunition boxes stored near the tent of a lieutenant with Averell's Cavalry at Westover Landing, Va., 1862.*

## Cut List

# AMMUNITION BOX

Overall Dimensions: 7⅞" x 12¼" x 16¼"

| Name | Qty. | Wood | Dimensions |
|------|------|------|------------|
| Sides | 2 | SPF | ¾" x 6⅜" x 16¼" (a) |
| Ends | 2 | SPF | ¾" x 6⅜" x 12¼" (a) |
| Lid/Bottom | 2 | SPF | ¾" x 12¼" x 16¼" (b) |
| Handles | 2 | SPF | 1" x 1" x 12¼" |
| Lid Cleats | 2 | SPF | ½" x 1" x 10¾" (c) |

Notes:

(a) Length includes box joints.

(b) Lid/Bottom dimensions are finished size.

(c) Inside width of box is 10¾", so cleats should be just slightly shorter.

*See drawing on page 59*

precise sizes and were bundled in packages of 10. To get exactly 1,000 cartridges into a standard box, the interior dimensions also had to be exact.

Everything else, however, seemed up to the whims of the individual arsenals, including wood thickness (which altered the exterior dimensions of the boxes), style and placement of the wooden handles, number and type of nails used, and any other markings on the box. Further, the arsenals frequently ignored every other specification except the interior dimensions and required markings. For example, they used just about any available wood in the SPF families, not just pine. There are numerous surviving ammo boxes from both sides of the war with rabbeted joints or even plain butt joints. Some boxes had full-width handles, others had short hand-grip handles; handle ends could be angled, rounded or just left square; handle placement was roughly centered, but it wasn't unusual to see handles anywhere from the center to the very top edge. In addition to the prescribed markings on the box ends and underside of the lid, some arsenals stenciled the top and both sides as well. Regulations called for the boxes to be painted, but there are numerous examples on both sides where painting was skipped. While unpainted boxes were far more common for the Confederates—especially later in the war—it's a myth that the North painted boxes and the South didn't.

It should also be pointed out that many of these construction and marking differences occurred within individual arsenals—I've examined Watervliet Arsenal boxes with angled dovetails, square dovetails (often called box joints), rabbet joints, and butt joints. The amount of information and the marking styles among those Watervliet boxes, as well as the size, shape and location of handles, is similarly all over the road.

*Interior view of Fort Johnson, Morris Island, S.C. These Confederate ammo boxes for artillery projectiles use simple butt joints, and have not been painted.*

This vast variety of styles gives a great deal of freedom when creating reproductions of ammo boxes—get the interior dimensions right, and you can be flexible pretty much everywhere else and still be correct.

## Getting started

The ammo box in this project is based on one I had the opportunity to examine a few years ago from the Watervliet Arsenal, made in 1862, and is fairly typical of those used on both sides for 1,000 cartridges for rifled muskets in the .57/.58 caliber range. The exact caliber depended on the rifle used, but the difference in musket ball size between the two calibers is so slight it can be ignored— both armies did, and issued specs for interior box dimensions that were the same for both calibers, at 14.75" long, 10.75" wide and 6.38" deep. The first two dimensions convert easily to match standard woodworking measures at 14¾" and 10¾"; the last

## MILITARY ARSENALS

There were several arsenals active during the Civil War. Many were originally U.S. arsenals, but became part of the Confederacy as their home states seceded from the Union. Others came into being during the war. A number changed hands as the Union captured them from Southern forces. Here's a sampling of arsenals to consider when marking ammo boxes.

### Union
Allegheny Arsenal (Pa.)
Benicia Arsenal (Calif.)
Frankford Arsenal (Pa.)
St. Louis Arsenal (Mo.)
Washington Arsenal (D.C.)
Watertown Arsenal (Mass.)
Watervliet Arsenal (N.Y.)

### Confederate
Charleston Arsenal (S.C.)
Columbia Arsenal (S.C.)
C.S. Laboratories (Ga.)
Harpers Ferry Arsenal (Va., later W.Va.)
Little Rock Arsenal (Ark.)
Richmond Arsenal (Va.)
Selma Arsenal (Ala.)

*A view of the Charleston Arsenal in South Carolina.*

LIBRARY OF CONGRESS

doesn't convert directly, but comes to just a hair under 6⅜". You can do the exact math if you want, but 6⅜" is fine.

I elected to use standard ¾" lumber for this project, but anything from ¾" to a full 1" is O.K. I've seen several surviving boxes with sides thicker than ¾", but none thinner that couldn't be attributed to general wood shrinkage. The part dimensions in the material list for this project are based on ¾" stock, but be sure to alter the lengths accordingly if you use thicker wood. For example, the box sides in this project are 16¼" long (14¾" + ¾" + ¾"). Increase the wood to 1", and the length must be 16¾" to give the correct interior dimensions. As mentioned earlier in the book, rough wood is better than smooth, so, unless you need to remove milling marks, avoid sanding if possible.

Start by cutting your components to length and width. The bottom and lid for this box are 12¼" wide. As with the hardtack crate, you'll be hard pressed to find a piece of stock wide enough to make the bottom and lid from a single piece, so plan to make these out of two pieces joined at the center with a tongue-and-groove joint.

## Box joinery

This ammo box uses simple dovetails with square pins and tails, more frequently called box joints. The easiest way to mark the exact cutting depth is to use a piece of the same stock you're using for the box. When cutting your components to length, first cut a short piece to use as a marking guide as in Fig. 1. With the guide, mark the ends of each component.

To mark the dovetail width, first lay all four sides end-to-end. Then draw lines across both pieces where the cutlines will be. (Fig. 2) The box sides have three *pins* on the end, while the end pieces have two *tails* spaced to match the pins. Again, 6⅜" doesn't divide evenly very well, but the best way to make everything come out right is to make the two

*Figure 1*

outside dovetails/cutouts 1¼", with the one in the center picking up the slack at 1⅜". (This isn't just a convenience for our purposes, by the way—original ammo boxes often had their dovetails, when used, very unevenly spaced.) To get all four corners marked, you'll need to move a workpiece from one end of your lineup to the other.

To make the dovetails fit together, you'll need to cut out every other one. The best way to keep this straight is to use a pencil to mark the spaces that are waste to be cut out as in Fig. 3. Next, cut out the waste areas of the dovetails. You can do this with a handsaw, jigsaw, on the tablesaw with a dado blade setup, on a router table with a straight bit, or on the

*Figure 3*

bandsaw as I've elected to do in Fig. 4. Whatever method you use, cut carefully just inside the line on the waste side, and not directly on the line. If you cut exactly on the line, your dovetails will be too loose to make a solid joint.

You'll notice that I've stacked two end pieces to cut at the same time, which is very easy to do on the bandsaw or with a handheld jigsaw. This is fine as long as you keep the workpieces together so they don't slide and throw off your cuts (clamping an edge will help), and as long as you keep the two components oriented correctly—top edges together at all times.

*Figure 2*

*Figure 4*

With all the cuts made, dry-assemble the box to check the fit. If a corner ends up a little tight and difficult to fit, it's easy to widen the cuts a bit with sandpaper till the joint slides together easily. You want a snug fit—not too loose, not too tight.

Original boxes would not have used glue on these corner joints, and if you've made the cuts so that you have a snug fit at each corner you won't need any either. However, feel free to use a bit of glue for a stronger box if you'd like.

With the box assembled, drive a nail through each pin and tail. In Fig. 5. I'm using 2" box nails, but anything up to 2½" is fine.

## Top and bottom

For the bottom and lid panels, construction is identical to that described for the Hardtack Crate in the previous chapter, so I won't repeat the instructions here. The bottom and lid panels of this ammo box are narrower than in the Hardtack Crate, so wood movement isn't as much of a concern. While the arsenals would generally not have used glue to join the two pieces making these panels, feel free to use glue if you'd like; since you'll want the lid

to remain in one piece glue for that panel may a be a good idea if you're willing to be slightly inauthentic.

Attach the bottom to your ammo box just as we did for the Hardtack Crate. Because I plan to carry a lot of stuff, I opted for 2½" nails, three down each side edge, and two on each end. To keep nail heads from scraping or catching, set them just below the surface with a nail set as in Fig. 6. Note the tongue-and-groove joint in the center of the bottom panel.

I've constructed the lid for the ammo box exactly like the one in the Hardtack Crate project in the last chapter, with cleats on the underside that keep the lid in place and center it on the box. Again, I won't repeat those instructions here. Inside cleats weren't used by the arsenals, so keep that in mind. (As with the Hardtack Crate, however, adding cleats to box lids was a common modification when soldiers adapted wooden boxes for other uses.)

These lids were originally fastened with screws, so for an authentic look you'll want to drive screws

*Figure 6*

in and then remove them to create visible holes. (Fig. 7) If you intend for your ammo box to look like an unopened box (that is, if the public is to think it's filled with cartridges and solidly sealed), drive the screws into place, remove them, and then cut them off where they protrude from the underside of the lid. This way you can leave the

*Figure 5*

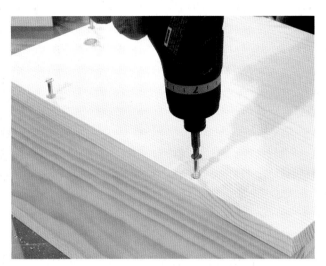

*Figure 7*

*Figure 8*

shortened screws in place for an authentic look, and still be able to remove the lid at any time.

The last construction detail is to add handles to each end. I made mine from some 1" x 1" pine cut to the 12¼" width of the box. As I mentioned before, the placement of these handles can be just about anywhere. I nailed mine in place about 1½" down from the top of the open box, but you can place yours higher or lower. You can also make the handles smaller than the box width if you wish; either is correct. I cut the corners of the handle off at an angle to eliminate the square corners, but this is optional.

The ordnance manuals call for the nails on these handles to be "clenched," more commonly today

called clinched. To do this, select a nail that will protrude through both handle and the box end by about ¼". For my box, a 2" nail did the trick. With the nail sticking out of the box interior, hammer it to one side then flatten it onto the inner wall. Then use a nail set to drive the bent-over nail tip just below the surface as shown in Fig. 8. This made for a very strong handle—those nails simply won't pull out—which is good considering that an original ammo box filled with 1,000 cartridges would weigh almost 100 lbs.

## Paint

If an ammo box was painted, it was done so with a color that denoted the type of ammunition it contained. Per the ordnance manuals for both North and South, a box for .57/.58-caliber cartridges was to be painted olive.

Now, exactly what this olive paint looked like is one of the livelier discussions (or arguments) among authentic reenactors on the various Civil War online forums. The exact formula for olive paint is in both ordnance manuals, but attempting to mix up a batch using modern approximations of the original ingredients isn't likely to produce an exact match to what it was then. And no surviving box, after nearly 150 years, even comes close to being the same color as on the day it was painted. For that matter, paint quickly changed color with use and exposure to the elements, so even back then a painted box didn't stay its original color very long. Add to that the fact that individual arsenals and contractors didn't always follow army specs exactly (sometimes they didn't even try), so it's impossible to pinpoint a so-called "authentic" olive paint.

Over the years, a lot of reenactors have come to an agreement—sort of—that a couple modern paints come close to what the original olive color probably looked like. The easiest of these to obtain is a color from Pittsburgh Paints called "Dock Piling." This color used to be commonly available at any store carrying Pittsburgh Paints products; just grab the color chip, go to the counter, and five minutes later you're out the door with a can of paint. The bad news is that Dock Piling has been discontinued. The good news is that the formula, #7631, is still in the computer at any Pittsburgh Paints location. It might take them a while for the clerk to find it, but it's in there.

When having the paint mixed up, you'll have your choice of paint type and sheen factor. The easiest paints to use today are latex paints, of course, but they used oil-based paint back then. Fortunately, you can get Dock Piling in either. For the highest authenticity, chose oil-based. (The fact is, however, that once it dries and you've used it out in the field, you cannot tell the difference between oil-based and latex; it looks the same.) For sheen, choose gloss or semi-gloss. Heavily pigmented paints of the period weren't that shiny—the more pigment you added to paint, the less gloss—so the latter may be the better choice.

Ammo boxes were not painted on the inside, so leave the inside unpainted. Also, the boxes where usually painted after the lids where screwed on, so for higher authenticity do likewise. The lid may stick a bit once removed and small amounts of paint may seep under the lid, but that's OK and perfectly authentic.

## Stenciling

I covered the steps for stenciling in Chapter 2, so I won't repeat them here.

When it comes to stenciling for ammo boxes (see the end of the chapter), remember that the army specs required only that the place and date of fabrication be marked on the underside of the lid, and the number and type of cartridges be marked on each end. Beyond that, there were dozens of variations, far too many to include here.

# AMMO BOX MARKINGS

From time to time, reenactors express interest in a generic ammo box, one that can be used in any Civil War setting. For the most part, there's no reason why a box made to basic army specs can't be used generically unless the reproduction is time- or place-specific. For example, stencil "May 1864" on the side of a box (yes, some had dates stenciled on the outside and not just under the lid), and you've ruled out using the box for a Gettysburg scenario.

Unfortunately, the myth that all Federal boxes were painted and all Confederate boxes were unpainted remains. While it's true that many Confederate boxes weren't painted, an olive-green box stenciled simply with, say, "1000 BALL CARTRIDGES" and ".58 CAL" could literally be from almost any arsenal on either side at any time during the war. The point is that a lot of original boxes already *were* generic. And if you're minimal with your markings, your reproduction box can fit in just about anywhere.

Ammo boxes were captured anytime one side or the other lost a battle. You can bet the Union army ended up with hundreds of full Rebel ammo boxes after Gettysburg, much as the Confederates did after Fredericksburg and Chancellorsville. Further, remember that ammo boxes were nothing more than castoffs and litter when empty, so it's perfectly fine for empty Union boxes to be used for seating and storage in a Reb camp, and vice-versa.

The less information included in stenciling, the more generic the box. A marking must include how many and what kind, but beyond that nothing more was required by army regs. With that in mind, here are some considerations.

A basic 1000 CARTRIDGES or 1000 BALL CARTRIDGES is fine. If the box is painted olive, it's implied that it contains ammunition for a RIFLE MUSKET, but that can be added if desired. (It should definitely be included on an unpainted box.)

Although some original boxes omitted ball size, most included it. This was usually abbreviated as .58 CAL or CAL. 58, but was spelled out on some boxes. The common spelling of the day was "CALIBRE," however, and not CALIBER. Calibers could be listed as .574, .577, .57 or .58 (with or without the period). Rifles of .58 caliber, such as the Springfield, could use any of those sizes so that rifle was only rarely specified on boxes. Although the .577 caliber British Enfield rifle could use the same .58 caliber ammunition made for the U.S. Springfield, boxes that contained true .577 caliber balls often had ENFIELD MUSKET stenciled on them. The powder charge in grains was also sometimes included, almost always abbreviated as GR.

Punctuation on ammo box markings ran the gamut. Some boxes included a period after abbreviations or before caliber sizes, others didn't. Commas and apostrophes were sometimes there, sometimes not.

Descriptive words for the ball were sometimes included. The word "EXPANDING" was sometimes spelled out but was usually abbreviated as EXP'D'G or EXPD'G. A number of box markings included the outline of an expanding ball instead of using the actual word. The word ELONGATED was sometimes included. More rarely, words like MINIE BULLET, DIAMETER (or DIAM.), FOR, and THE were included, but these were not common and are probably best avoided unless you are copying a specific original box. In addition, decorative flourishes were sometimes used on the ends of descriptive lines, but these were not particularly common.

Speaking of abbreviations, CARTRIDGES was sometimes shortened to CART, CART'G or CARTG and was sometimes spelled as "CARTRGs" with the smaller "s" set above a period. The same goes for "MUSKt," with the small "t"—either in upper or lowercase"—set above a period. When it came to rules regarding abbreviations, there didn't seem to be any.

I've included stencils that match the Watervliet box I saw, but making your own is simply a matter of deciding upon an arsenal, a date, and the type of ammunition. Text was generally a Roman font, measuring about ¾" high. I've included a list of arsenals in a sidebar appearing on page 52. Your

box, it could go on any flat surface, and they weren't always particular about getting it on straight. They weren't always particularly careful, either, and there are numerous examples in photos and surviving boxes showing some truly sloppy paint jobs, so don't feel you have to make your stenciling perfect.

On painted boxes they most often used white paint for visibility when stenciling, but there are some less-common examples that used both black and white. For unpainted boxes—and for the raw wood on the underside of the lids—black paint was the usual choice.

*Not all reenactors portray soldiers. Ken Knott, shown here in front of his tent displaying his wares, does a mortician impression at reenactments and Living History events.*

## Final touch

One last detail from the ordnance manuals is to line the boxes with paper. The regs don't specify, but this was likely a heavy, sized paper that was somewhat water-resistant. The paper would be cut in two pieces, with each piece long enough so that once lining the inner box surfaces, the ends would serve as flaps that folded over the top of the cartridge packages.

To date, I have yet to see an extant ammo box that still has this paper lining. My guess is that this paper lining was either not physically attached to the inner surfaces, or was adhered with a very mild adhesive such as paste or mucilage that would allow the paper to pull free rather easily. Of course, those could be yet another of the specs the arsenals didn't follow in many cases, especially later in the war. Unless you plan to use your ammo box for display in which it is filled with 1,000 cartridges exactly as it may have appeared fresh from the arsenal, it's probably a detail you can skip.

As we've seen, ignoring Army specifications is often very period-correct.

best bet for making a specific box is to use an Internet search engine such as Google to find one; original ammo boxes pop up frequently at relic dealers, and are relatively easy to find.

Like painting, stenciling was done after the lid was attached (except for the date and arsenal location under the lid, of course), and the arsenals considered all flat surfaces to be a canvas. End-of-box stenciling could go just below the handle; both above and below the handle; or above, below, *and* on the handle itself. Stenciling was done that sometimes overlapped the ends of the lid, and stenciling was sometimes done lazily in that the ends or beginnings of words ran off the edges of the box. Basically, if they had information to put on the

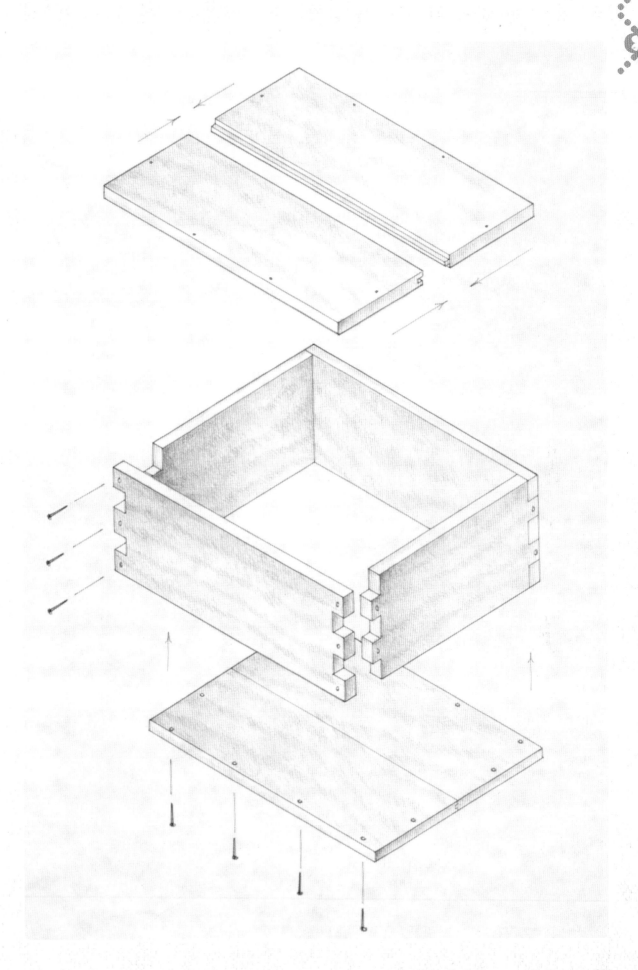

**1000 BALL CARTRIDGES**

**RIFLE MUSKET CAL. 57, 65 GR.**

*Use an enlarging copier or scan this stencil to create a printout of working size. Regardless of the overall size of the stencil, the text portion should measure approximately 5½" high by 10" wide (letters should be about ¾" tall).*

# WATERVLIET ARSENAL APR, 1862

*Use an enlarging copier or scan this stencil to create a printout of working size. Regardless of the overall size of the stencil, the text portion should measure approximately 3¼" high by 7⅜" wide (letters should be about ¾" tall).*

# Chapter 6:
# FOLDING CAMP TABLE

While the privates usually made do with what they could find for a table—an inverted hardtack crate, or maybe a board or two balanced across a stump—more elaborate camp furniture in the field was common for the higher ranks. Some of this furniture the officers brought from home or picked up in towns as the forces moved. Unlike the privates, corporals, and sergeants who carried just about everything they used on their backs, an officer's gear was carried in wagons so it was easier for them to travel with tables, chairs, beds, carpets and a host of other amenities. Rank indeed had its privileges.

But whenever the troops stopped for any length of time in the middle of nowhere, it wasn't unusual for officers to have furniture made for them in the field. (If the army was camped for an extended period of time, such as in winter quarters, privates experienced in carpentry would do the same for themselves.) The Five-Board Bench project in Chapter 3 is a good example, as is this simple folding camp table.

## *Cut List*

## FOLDING CAMP TABLE

Overall Dimensions: 22" x 29", standing 32" high

| Name | Qty. | Wood | Dimensions |
|---|---|---|---|
| Tabletop | 1 | SPF | ¾" x 22" x 29" |
| Tabletop Braces | 2 | SPF | ¾" x 2½" x 22" |
| Legs | 4 | SPF | ¾" x 2½" x 37" |
| Leg Stretchers | 2 | SPF | ¾" x 2" x 25½" |
| Upper Stretcher | 1 | SPF | ¾" x 2" x 24" |
| Stop Block | 1 | SPF | 1" x 1" x 12" |
| Dowels | 2 | SPF | ¾" x 1½" |
| Dowels | 2 | SPF | ¾" x 2½" |

*See drawing on page 71*

I used the marvelous photos on page 63 from the National Archives and the Library of Congress as a guide for this project. The photos show two officers of the 179th N.Y. infantry regiment, which fought at Cold Harbor, and took part in the siege of Petersburg and Appomattox campaign. As you can see, their tent has quite a few comforts: a wooden floor, a real bed with plenty of blankets (no idea whose foot that is sticking out from under the covers in the one photo), and a folding table.

The function of a table of this type is very basic. A pair of legs on each side is joined scissor-style at the center with either a short dowel or, as it appears in this photo, a longer square rod. In this latter method the square rod joins each pair of legs across the table's span, slipping through squared holes in the center of each leg set. A peg is then inserted through a small hole in the ends of the rod to secure it. Because the rod spans the table width, it lends rigidity to the structure as well. This method does not allow the legs to pivot; to fold up the table, the pegs are removed, the rod slipped out, and the table collapsed. Obviously, this method takes longer to set up or store the table—and also results in several separate, loose pieces—so it was generally used when a table was going to stay put for a while. It's likely these photos were taken at Petersburg where the Union Army sat for many months during the siege of the city, so a table like that makes sense.

The dowel method allows the table to be folded down and carried as a single unit—no loose pieces. A short dowel joined the legs together where they cross, creating a pivot. No solid rod spans the table, so rigidity is achieved with stretchers on the lower portion of the legs. This method is more versatile (and doesn't require cutting square holes), so I've used it in this project.

In both methods the leg pairs are attached to the table top on one or both sides by means of dowels through the tabletop braces. This keeps the legs firmly attached, but allows the table to be collapsed and folded up for transport. I've elected to

## SEEING DOUBLE

So what's with the two nearly identical photos at the beginning of this project?

Wet-plate photography was fairly new at the time of the Civil War, only about a decade old. As a result, having a picture taken was an exciting novelty and photographers followed the troops just about everywhere.

Frequently when a photographer shot a photo of a particular scene he did the same thing we do today: To be sure at least one good image came out, he took more than one. It wasn't unusual for the subjects of these multiple photos to change positions and even take turns being the main subject.

Such was the case with this camp scene with the 179th N.Y. regiment. It's obvious the photos were taken back-to-back—note that the corner of the bed sheet doesn't change at all, and the straw hat on the table doesn't move. Each of the officers is holding a cigar. Who knows? It might be the same one in both photos.

Multiple photos of the same scene are a boon to historians, researchers and, of course, woodworkers. I was lucky enough to find three versions of the photo for the Lt. Kelly Camp Chair project later in the book. Having the three distinct views allowed me to see details of the chair I never could have gotten from a single photo. It was the next best thing to being there.

attach them with dowels on one side only, and to use an upper stretcher and stop-block on the other side.

## Stock preparation

The stock used for the officers' table in the photos appears to be ¾" or very close to it, so we'll use standard home-center lumber for the project. Feel free to use something a bit thicker if you'd like. I couldn't get any measurements from either of these gentlemen, of course, but a table 22" x 29" looked about right. Remember, this isn't an item with standard specifications like the Ammo Box project, so feel free to change any of the dimensions for this table to suit your needs.

Like most field-made items, this table was undoubtedly made of something in the SPF families, so I've selected pine for this project. Tables of this type could have been made with hardwood, but keep in mind that woods like oak and maple would have been harder to work in the field by hand.

As with all projects where you'll take most components from the same board, cut your larger pieces, like those for the tabletop, first. Since the legs and tabletop braces are the same width, the stock for them can all be ripped to width at the same time, then cut to length as needed. (Fig. 1)

The tabletop braces on the table in the photographs are notched to eliminate the sharp corners. I elected to do the same, but these braces could be rounded on the ends instead. The exact size of this notch isn't critical, but I measured about 1¼" from the corner on each side, marked the brace and cut across it.

Even though only two of the legs require dowels at the top, all four need to be fully or partially rounded on the upper ends to allow them to swing freely under the tabletop when folding. The lower ends will be cut at an angle to firmly meet the ground. Since the legs here are 2½" wide, the pivot

point is 1¼" from the sides and end. By marking all four legs, you'll find the pivot points needed to center the dowel holes as well as the necessary cutlines for rounding them. The pivot point on one end of each brace is offset 2" from the end. (Fig. 2)

The legs that will be drilled for the dowel will pivot in only one direction to fold the table, and so only need to be rounded on one side. The other pair of legs should be rounded at the top on both sides. Using a ¾" bit, drill the holes in one end

Figure 1

Figure 2

*Figure 3*

*Figure 4*

of the braces as in Fig. 3. I did this on the drill press, but you can also use a hand drill. Drill the matching holes in the tops of the two legs that are half-rounded.

## Assembly

Mark a line about 1⅜" from both ends of the boards that will make up the tabletop; this will be the nailing line for the braces underneath. Aligning the braces exactly centered on the line from underneath is easier if you first cut a spacer. I cut a piece of scrap to 1" wide for the spacer, which perfectly centers the ¾"-thick braces on the nailing line. Remember that you'll need to adjust the width of your spacer if you use lumber other than ¾" thick. Put the top boards together edge-to-edge—do not edge-glue them—and temporarily clamp the spacer to the ends. (This also holds the top together to make nailing easier.) Set the clamped top on the braces, sliding the brace up against the spacer, and drive three 2" to 2½" nails through each board and into the brace underneath as in Fig. 4. When nailing on the end with the dowel hole, be careful to place

the nail so that it misses the hole. Repeat with the brace on the other side and unclamp the spacer.

We didn't edge-glue the top together, and that's important. A solid 22"-wide panel would surely crack when it expands and contracts with changes in seasonal humidity, but leaving the top as two separate 11"-wide boards will allow for movement. In fact, you'll notice that in cold, dry weather a gap will appear between the two boards; it'll probably close up in the summer.

I've sized the legs to create a table that stands about 32" high. To adjust the height, here's a non-Pythagorean-math way to get the correct leg length. Lay the completed tabletop upside down against a 90-degree surface—your refrigerator is a perfect spot. Measure up the vertical surface and make a mark at the desired table height. (If you're using your refrigerator, pencil is a good idea.) Measure from this mark to the center of the pivot point where the leg will attach. Add 1¼" and you've got your new leg length.

*Figure 5*

I've already cut the correct angle for the leg bottom in Fig. 5, but to find it easily for one of a different length simply attach the leg at the pivot point and lean it up against the refrigerator again. Hold a square against the refrigerator where the leg makes contact, and use the square as a guide to draw a line across the leg bottom from this point at 90 degrees to the refrigerator, and there you go. Without using either math or a protractor you've got the perfect angle for the leg bottom.

The next step is to find the correct anchor point for the leg sets on the other side of the table. Put the legs from each side of the table together and drill a ¾" dowel hole in the center for the pivot points there. Slip a short length of dowel into the center of the leg set, and with the tabletop upside down on a flat surface attach the leg with the doweled top to the table. Use some clamps to hold everything and adjust the leg set until the bottoms (which are now pointed up, remember) are in a level plane, as I've done in Fig. 6 using a straightedge.

Because the inner legs are offset by the width of the outer legs, there's a ¾" gap between the inner leg and the tabletop brace. Slip a piece of ¾" scrap

into this gap and clamp the leg in place as in Fig. 7. This will allow you to mark the upper stretcher exactly for cutting. If you've opted to make the table 29" long, the upper stretcher should be about 24", but doing it this way will give you an exact measurement if you're a little off. It's important that this piece be the correct length, as it will need to slip inside the outer legs when the table is folded. At this time, also mark the position where it should be attached on the upper legs.

While you hold the upper stretcher in place, position the stop block on the underside of the tabletop and mark its position as well. I used a

*Figure 6*

*Figure 7*

Figure 8

the table much sturdier than the square rod in the photos would have.

Slip out the dowels holding the legs to the tabletop, then fold up the legs as a unit and lay it on a flat surface. Lay one of the stretchers across the lower legs and nail it into place about 6" or 7" from the bottom. (Fig. 9) Because this is a major structural point for the table, I recommend using glue and 2½" nails. Flip the leg set over and attach the other stretcher in the same way.

Up until now I've been using short dowel scraps during construction. If you haven't already, cut two ¾" dowels to 1½" long and slip them into place at the center leg pivots. Drill a pilot hole through the edge of one of the legs on each side and into the

short piece of leftover 1"-thick pine from when I made the handles for the Ammo Box project, but you can use just about any piece of pine scrap you have lying around. The exact width, thickness and length aren't critical, but the piece needs to be thick enough to keep the upper stretcher in place when the table is in the upright position.

Cut the upper stretcher to length as in Fig. 8 and nail it in place at the top of the legs on the marks you made in the previous step using 2" to 2½" nails. At this point also attach the stop block to the underside of the tabletop. They would probably have not used glue for this in the field, but I recommend it here. I used 1½" nails for the stop block, but choose your nail length carefully to match the dimensions of your stop block so the nails don't go all the way through the tabletop. You can use screws for this instead if you wish.

The table is now ready to try out. Flip it right side up and check that all the legs have clearance and that the upper stretcher rests securely against the tabletop stop block. If you get some rubbing in the legs, ease the fit with sandpaper. You'll notice at this point that the table is a bit wobbly, which is to be expected. If we had used the square-rod method I described earlier, it would be a bit steadier, but not to worry. We're going to add a pair of stretchers to the lower ends of the legs that will actually make

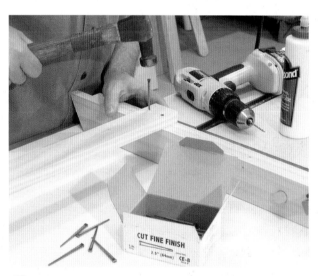

Figure 9

dowel, then drive a 1½" nail into the hole to secure the dowel. I did this on the inner legs, but it doesn't matter whether you choose the inner or outer leg, just be sure not to do both or the legs won't pivot.

Now, I probably would have done the same thing with the dowels that attach the upper legs to the tabletop braces. However, I can see in both photos that the dowel in this location is fairly long, and there's a loop of string on it. I'm not completely sure why they would have done this, but when I got to thinking about it, it occurred to me that making the tabletop readily detachable could have some benefits. For one thing, it would make the table easier to repair if one of the legs had to be replaced. The biggest advantage, though, is that it would allow the tabletop to be used independently of the legs, meaning that it could be set up across a tree stump or other temporary support in the field, or perhaps used as a tray. This is just a guess, of course, but I liked the idea so I've done the same with this table.

Cut two dowels about 2" long, and drill a small hole across the end of each. Thread a piece of heavy string or twine (100% cotton, linen or hemp, of course; no synthetics) through the hole and tie it in a loop, and then slip the dowels into place. If you take the tabletop off, you can hang those dowels over the top of the leg to keep track of them.

## Variations

The most obvious variation on this table is to change the size, which you should feel free to do. Same thing with the stock thickness, although I wouldn't go any thinner than ⅝". As far as stock width, I attempted here to match the size of the table in the photos as closely as possibly and so used 2½" wide material for the legs and tabletop braces. However, 2"-wide stock would probably be fine for softwood, and down to 1½" for hardwood.

For use as a field or camp item, stick with wood from the SPF families, but if you'd like to make the table for other use, you can substitute hardwood for a stronger, longer-lasting table. Poplar and oak are good choices.

Instead of using removable dowels to attach the tabletop, set the dowels permanently in the leg top the same way we did the dowels at the center pivots.

I used a piece of 2"-wide stock to create the upper stretcher. You could instead use a dowel here that runs the width of the table, set into each upper leg through holes. This dowel stretcher can rest against the same type of simple block we used here, or you can attach a pair of narrow cleats with a rounded notch cut into them instead. The dowel would rest in the rounded notches, making for a somewhat sturdier table.

You don't even have to use an upper stretcher at all if you don't want to. Instead of an upper stretcher and stop block under the table, you could instead attach the upper legs with dowels just as we did on the other side. Remember that the inner leg tops are offset by ¾" from the tabletop brace, so you'll need to attach a spacer to fill the gap before drilling holes for the dowels. That side of the table isn't visible in the photos, so there's no way to tell just how those legs were attached.

Finally, this table has angled leg bottoms to match the one in the photo. However, you could round the bottoms instead, or even just leave them cut square; either way would still be period-correct.

*Ian McWherter* (center), *a reenactor with "The Fighting Boys Mess," looks pleased with his hand, while David Rodgers* (left) *and Don Smith, both with the 1st Calif. Infantry, appear not to have enjoyed the luck of the draw.*

# Chapter 7:
# BUCKSAW

When it came to preparing firewood, the two main tools in the 19th century were the axe and bucksaw. Sawing logs to shorter length was called *bucking*, hence the name bucksaw. (The sawhorse-like stand used to hold a log for bucking is called a *sawbuck*.) The bucksaw isn't specific to the Civil War, of course—it predated it by centuries—but it was one of the most common tools that traveled with the soldiers on campaign.

A bucksaw is pretty much the same thing as a bow saw, except it's beefier and heavier-duty due to its main task of cutting logs. Bow saws are usually lighter with very thin blades, and are used for fine cutting for furniture making and other woodworking.

Like the soldiers during the war, modern-day reenactors have a constant need for firewood at events. Firewood is almost always supplied by event organizers—usually dumped unceremoniously by truck in some central location—but this wood is on a strict first-come basis. Inevitably, it runs out and reenactors resort to digging through the woods to find more. A bucksaw can not only come in incredibly handy for this task, but using one in camp is an excellent way to give a Living History demonstration for spectators.

You might even find that you like using this saw around the shop and yard. It's very versatile and easy to use, plus making your own woodworking tools can instill a sense of pride almost as great as that achieved by woodworking itself.

I should mention up front that I've made a compromise with the blade I've used for this bucksaw project. It's strictly a modern blade that's not as wide as those used on old saws, and it features a tooth pattern different from that used back then. However, you'll be very hard-pressed to find a wider blade that resembles an original; even if you locate one, the metal composition and tooth pattern still won't be a match. You can, of course, scour antique shops for old blades, but they're likely to be fairly rusty and unusable. Even if they can be cleaned up enough to press them into service, you'll find that they just don't cut very well at all. Believe me, I've tried. Modern bucksaw blades cut very well indeed, and with use quickly take on a well-used patina.

You can buy bucksaw blades today in six standard lengths: 12", 18", 21", 24", 30" and 36". Because the 21" blade is the most commonly available, I've designed this project to use that size. Feel free to alter the dimensions of the saw to use any other size blade you like, however, simply by adjusting the length of the center stretcher on the saw.

## *Cut List*

# BUCKSAW

Overall Dimensions: 16" x 22⅜"

| Name | Qty. | Wood | Dimensions |
|------|------|------|------------|
| Handles | 2 | Oak | ¾" x 3" x 16" (a) |
| Stretcher | 1 | Oak | ¾" x 1½" x 18" (b) |
| Winding Paddle | 1 | Oak | ¼" x 1½" x 7½" |

**Notes:**

(a) Dimensions listed are for stock before cutting handle profiles.

(b) Listed length of stretcher does not include tenons.

*See handle pattern on page 79*

*Figure 1*

## Getting started

For this project, you'll want to use a good hardwood—it's possible to make a bucksaw out of softwood, but you'd have to use pretty thick lumber for strength as the components are under a lot of stress when the blade is mounted and tightened. I've chosen oak, but hickory and ash were also commonly used. Cherry or some figured maple (maybe tiger maple or bird's-eye maple) would also make for a handsome saw. This is one of those times when common ¾" is the perfect thickness of wood to use, but anything from ¾" to 1" thick will work fine.

This bucksaw features mortise-and-tenon joinery for the stretcher. These joints are among the strongest around, which is good for the amount of stress put on the saw when it's under tension and being used. When working with this type of joinery, it's generally best to cut the mortise before the tenon, as the tenon is a bit more adjustable "after the fact" if you don't get things quite right.

Cut the workpieces for the handles, then draw the outline of the handles onto them. Note the flat area on the inside surface of the handles; this is where the mortise will be cut, forming a seat for the stretcher. Be sure when drawing the handle outline that this flat spot matches the stretcher width, and that it's perfectly parallel to the outside edge of the workpiece.

Cut out the outline for what will be the inside edge of the handle. (You'll want the outside edge of

the handle to remain flat until after you've cut the mortise.) I've used the bandsaw a lot so far for the projects, so this time I clamped the workpiece to my bench and used a jigsaw to cut the profile as in Fig. 1. You can use a bandsaw, jigsaw or scrollsaw, or you can take the hand-tool route and cut the handle out with a coping saw. Cut just outside the line and take care that the flat spot in the center of the handle remains flat and smooth, as that's where you'll cut the mortise in the next step. With the inside profile of the handle cut, sand the surface smooth; a spindle sander or sanding drum on the drill press works great for this.

## Mortise and tenon

Lay out the area for a ¾"-deep mortise that is ¼" wide by 1" long, centered in the flat spot on the inside of the handle. You can use a plunge router or a router table to cut mortises, but a benchtop hollow-chisel mortiser is the best, easiest way to do it—it's just like drilling a square hole. It uses a square, hollow chisel housing a drill bit that extends just beyond the end of the chisel. The drill bit clears a path, while the chisel cleans and squares up the inside surfaces of the mortise. Make a series of overlapping plunges into the workpiece until the length of the mortise is right. (Fig. 2) I'm using a

*Figure 2*

*Figure 3*

*Figure 4*

¼" hollow-chisel bit, so the width of the mortise is guaranteed to be right on the money. You can see now why I only had you cut the inside profile of the handle—the flat back allows you to firmly clamp the workpiece in place as you use the mortiser.

Alternatively, you can use a regular drill and chisel to cut the mortise. Drill a series of overlapping ¼" holes ¾" deep the length of the mortise (a Forstner bit works best for this), then clean up the sides and square the corners with a freshly sharpened bench chisel as in Fig. 3. Go slowly and carefully, measuring frequently to ensure the mortise is ¼" wide.

With both mortises cut, go ahead and cut the remainder of the handle outline, and do any sanding needed to smooth the handle profile.

*Figure 5*

Again, take care that the flat area at the mortise site remains perfectly flat.

Next, cut the tenons on the ends of the stretcher that will fit the mortises. Measure the stretcher and make your marks for the tenon carefully. The overall length of the stretcher includes the tenons on each end, but it's the distance between the shoulders of the tenons that determines how far apart the handles are. The shoulders of the tenon should be 18" apart to accommodate a 21" blade. If you've opted to use a blade of a different length, now is the time to alter the length of the stretcher.

Getting a tenon exactly right to fit a mortise can be tricky, so when you cut your stretcher to thickness and width, cut an extra length of the same material to the same width and thickness. Use this extra as a test piece to get the tenon just right before attempting to cut the tenon on the actual workpiece.

Tenons can be cut on the tablesaw with a tenoning jig or a dado set—and can be cut with a handsaw, of course—but we'll use the router table for this project. Adjust the height of your router bit to give you a tenon of the correct thickness—for ¾" stock, that means set the height at ¼". Taking multiple passes over the bit, cut the tenon on your marks as in Fig. 4. Note how I'm using a square backer-board to push the tenon across the bit; this keeps the stretcher at 90 degrees to the router table's fence, and helps prevent tear-out on the back of the stretcher.

Check the tenon fit as in Fig 5. If the tenon doesn't fit the mortise, adjust the bit accordingly. If the tenon's too small, lower the bit; if it's too big, raise it. Make your adjustments in very small increments, as it's easy to go past the correct height. Cut the end of the test piece off squarely and try again. When it makes a good fit—solid, but easy to slide in and out—the router is set perfectly and you're ready to cut the tenons on the real workpiece.

## Blade mounting and assembly

To find the mounting points for the saw blade, clamp the saw together at the stretcher, then lay the blade across the bottoms of the handles. (Fig. 6) A piece of scrap the same thickness as your workpieces will keep the blade from sagging while you mark the bottoms of the handles at the center of the blade's mounting holes. If your blade has more than one hole on the ends, use the hole closest to the center of the handle. Drill a ⅛" to ³⁄₁₆" hole completely through the handle.

The saw blade needs somewhere to go, so cut slots about 1½" deep centered in the bottom of each handle. These slots should match as closely as possible the thickness of the blade you plan to use, and can be cut by hand, with a scrollsaw, or on the bandsaw, as I've done in Fig. 7. (The blade of your jigsaw or tablesaw is too thick.)

Cut the winding paddle to size. The paddle can be the same thickness as the stock you use for the rest of the bucksaw, but a thinner paddle is easier to handle when winding and gives the saw a narrower profile. The paddle here is ¼" thick, but ⅜" to ½" is fine. Center it on the stretcher and mark the stretcher for a shallow notch that will keep the paddle in place. Because the paddle rests against the stretcher at an angle, I cut this notch at a slight angle so it fits firmly. (Fig. 8)

The last thing to do before assembling the bucksaw is to cut the tensioning cord. An 8' length will allow you to loop it around the upper handles twice before tying it off. The cord can be heavy string or twine or, if you prefer, strong leather.

To assemble, slip the handles onto the ends of the stretcher, then slide the blade into place in the handle slots. Be sure the holes in the blade ends line up with the holes you drilled earlier in the handle

*Figure 6*

*Figure 7*

*Figure 8*

bottoms. Slip a nail through each hole to hold the blade in place. I used a couple 1" cut hinge hails for this, but any cut headed nail will do. It's OK if the nail feels loose; once the saw is tensioned it won't go anywhere. The nails will stick out the other side for now, but we'll take care of this shortly.

Loop the cord around the upper handles and tie it securely with a square knot. The tighter the cord fits on the saw now, the less winding you'll

*Figure 9*

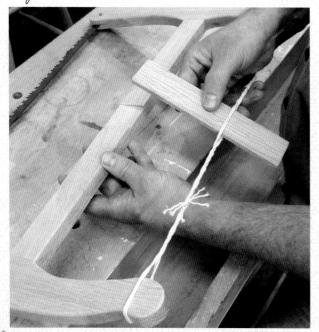

have to do to tension the saw. With the ends of the tied cord resting in the indentations on the outside profile of the upper handles, slip the winding paddle through the center of the looped cord and start winding as in Fig. 9. Be sure to wind in the direction that will keep the paddle resting in the stretcher notch, and continue winding until the blade is taut and the entire saw feels firm and solid. When everything is taut, pull the winding paddle toward the stretcher so it can engage the notch, and drop it into place.

With diagonal pliers, clip the protruding points off the two nails holding the blade flush with the side of the handle. You may wish to disassemble the saw, then take the nails out and round off the clipped ends with sandpaper or a file so no sharp edges stick out.

Give the saw a good sanding all around, especially on the lower portion of the handles where you'll hold it during use. If you wish, you can round this portion with a sanding block, drawknife or spokeshave into a handle shape for a comfortable grip. Rounding over the upper parts of the handles where the cord wraps around will add life to the cord.

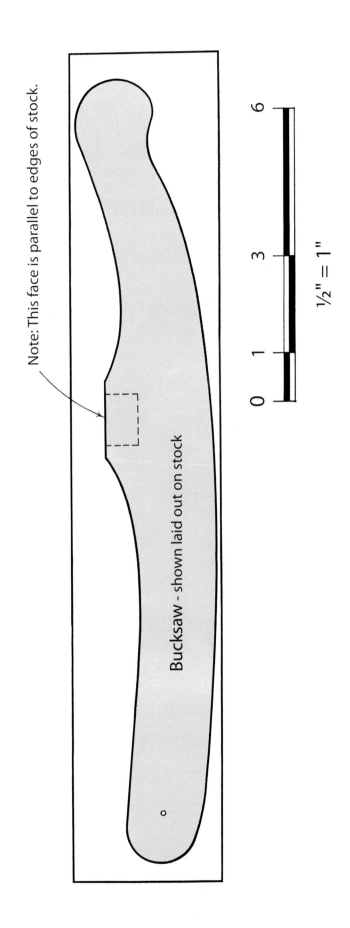

Note: This face is parallel to edges of stock.

Bucksaw - shown laid out on stock

0    1    3    6

½" = 1"

# *Chapter 8:*
# FOLDING CAMP STOOL

I mentioned early on that there are a number of things in reenacting that are over-represented. These things aren't necessarily inauthentic or incorrect, as proven by surviving examples and the photographic record. But when you examine historical photos carefully, it's clear that some just didn't occur during the Civil War in the same numbers as they seem to in reenacting and Living History presentations.

Few things are more over-represented than a particularly ubiquitous folding camp stool. No matter where you go, the stool's the same: It's made of light-colored oak, with rectangular legs measuring ¾" thick and 1" or 1¼" wide, and a light canvas seat. Reenacting suppliers have made this stool by the thousands, it seems, because it's everywhere. Again, it's not incorrect, but there are just too many of this same exact stool. You'll see some of them in the photographic record, but far more often you'll see stools with turned legs, curved legs, dark legs and tapestry seats.

*Engineers at Army of the Potomac headquarters, Petersburg, Va., 1864.*

## Cut List

# FOLDING CAMP STOOL

Overall Dimensions: 15" x 15", standing approximately 17½" high

| Name | Qty. | Wood | Dimensions |
|------|------|------|------------|
| Legs | 4 | Walnut | ¾" x 1⅝" x 22" |
| Rung/Inner Leg Set | 1 | Walnut/Oak | ¾" x 12⅛" |
| Rung/Outer Leg Set | 1 | Walnut/Oak | ¾" x 13⅜" |

**Note:** The overall dimensions of your stool will vary depending on the length and placement of the seat fabric. Also, over time the seat fabric will stretch, making the stool somewhat wider and lower.

*See drawing on page 90, and pattern on page 91*

Figure 1

When I decided to include a camp stool in this book, I was determined to avoid this too-common stool in favor of one more accurately matching surviving samples and the photographic record. Although I have an original turned-leg stool in my collection, I was a bit concerned about it's complexity as a project so I kept looking for something else.

I saw an interesting curved-leg stool in a museum, with walnut legs and a threadbare tapestry seat. It was perfect, but I couldn't tie it to the correct period. Not long afterward, I saw a photo of a nearly identical stool posted on one of the Civil War Internet forums. Once again I thought it was just right, but I still needed to make a firm connection to the period.

The Library of Congress came to my rescue. After several weeks of sifting through images I found it in this chapter's lead photo. The photo was shot in Petersburg in 1864, and shows a group of engineers and draftsmen at the Army of the Potomac headquarters. You can see one of the turned-leg stools in the foreground, but look over on the right side by the tent. There it was! I had my connection.

## Getting started

I used ⅞" walnut for the stool in this project, but ¾" is fine, so all the dimensions will reflect that throughout the project. You can use stock up to 1" thick, but that would just make for a heavier stool without adding appreciable strength. Stick with hardwood, however, or you'll definitely need thicker stock. Be sure to alter workpiece dimensions as needed if you use any thickness other than ¾".

This is the first piece of furniture so far in the book that's not field-made. A stool like this type would have been made in a cabinet shop in a small town, or may have been mass-produced. In either case there would not have been milling marks of any kind on the finished piece. Feel free to sand all surfaces smooth.

Cut out a leg pattern from stiff paper and use it to transfer the leg outline to your workpiece, orienting the curve of the leg with any curve occurring in the grain. In Fig. 1, I've used a bit of mineral spirits to make the grain more visible, and you can see that I've drawn the outline of the leg so it follows the grain closely. Using the natural grain flow in this way will make for stronger legs, but don't worry if you stock has perfectly straight grain; it'll still be plenty strong.

Figure 2

Figure 3

Cut out the legs with a jigsaw, scrollsaw, by hand or on the bandsaw, as in Fig. 2. A spindle sander makes quick work of the inside curve of the leg, while a disk sander takes care of the outside curve. (Fig. 3) Any hand sander can also be used. If you ever plan to make a second stool, it's a good idea to cut an extra leg to keep on hand to use as a template for making more legs. (Fig. 4)

## Construct the leg sets

We'll make the legs in two sets—an inner set and an outer set; one fits inside the other, riveted at a center pivot point, to make the stool.

Mark all four legs for the rungs and rivet holes by laying the pattern on the leg and punching directly through the paper with an awl or other pointed tool as in Fig. 5. Drill a ¾" hole ½" deep for each of the rungs. In Fig. 6, I'm using a drill press, which gives exact 90-degree holes, but you can use a hand drill if you're careful to keep the drill perfectly straight. Because the depth of this hole combined with the rung length determines the width of the finished leg sets, you may want to drill some test holes in scrap of the same thickness first until you have the depth exactly right. Change over to a ¼" drill bit and drill the holes for the rivets all the way through each of the four legs.

Remember that one leg set must be sized to exactly fit inside the other, so make the sets one at

Figure 4

Figure 5

Figure 6

Figure 7

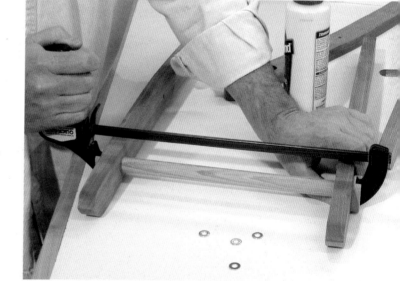

Figure 8

a time so you can adjust the second set to account for any slight errors in cutting. Start with the outer leg set by preparing the dowel for glue-up. When gluing dowel rungs, glue squeeze-out can be a problem. I like to round over the bottom edge of the dowel with a sanding block and cut a cross-hatch into it about $\frac{1}{16}$" deep as you can see in Fig. 7. This not only gives the glue someplace to go when clamping, but it also increases the gluing surface, making for a stronger joint.

Glue the legs onto the dowel rung and press together, then lay the leg set on a flat surface and check that both legs are in the exact same plane by making sure that all four legs tips contact the surface as indicated by my pencil in Fig. 8. Adjust as necessary and, keeping the leg tips flat on the surface, clamp up the leg set till dry. (Fig. 9)

Figure 9

While the outer leg set is clamped up, dry-assemble the inner leg set and place it inside the other to check for size. The inner leg set should be small enough to fit within the outer set with enough room on each side to slip a washer in the gap—about ¼₆". If your gap is too large, cut a new dowel rung slightly larger; if the gap is too small or if the inner leg set won't slip inside the other set, trim the dowel rung a bit at a time until the dry-assembled leg set fits correctly. Once you're satisfied that the inner leg set is right, glue the dowel rung in place and clamp up as before.

## Take a seat

Cut the seat braces to size. For comfortable seating and to make the tapestry seat wrap smoothly around them, we'll round the two top edges of the braces on the router table using, appropriately, a roundover bit. (Fig. 10) Run the first edge of one of the seat braces from right to left over the bit, flip the workpiece end-for end, and run the other side through. (Fig. 11) Repeat with the second brace. When you're

*Figure 10*

*Figure 11*

*Figure 12*

*Figure 13*

done, you'll have a nicely rounded seat brace, as in Fig. 12. Sand both braces smooth to remove any milling marks from the router table.

The tops of the four legs are set into dadoes on the underside of the seat braces. To get the exact location for these dados, lay each leg set at the rung on top of a brace and mark the locations. (Fig. 13) (The leg sets are different sizes, remember, so their respective dadoes will be located in different spots.) The dadoes for the seat braces can be made on a router table with a straight bit, on the tablesaw with a dado blade, or with a regular blade. If we were doing a lot of dadoes, I'd take the trouble to change the tablesaw over to a dado set, but since we're only making four I've left the regular blade in place. Set

*Figure 14*

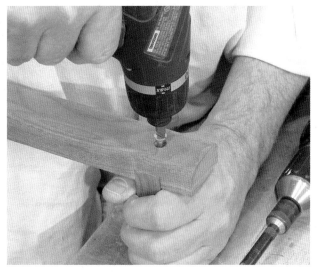

*Figure 15*

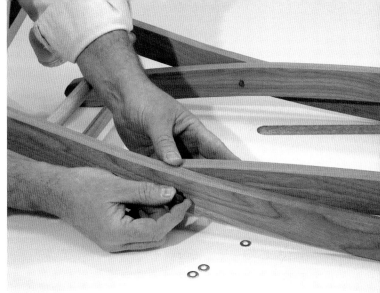

*Figure 16*

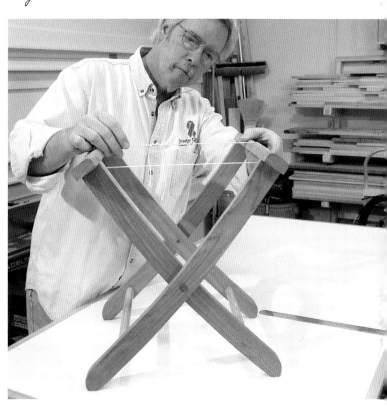

*Figure 17*

the blade height to ⅜" and, using a miter gauge, make the outermost cuts of the dado first, then just nibble away at the material in the center of the dado with multiple passes over the blade as in Fig. 14.

Mount the leg set in your vise and put the seat brace in place. Drill a countersunk pilot hole and attach the seat brace with a #10 x 1½" slotted flathead screw. (Fig. 15) I've used brass screws, but plain steel is fine. Repeat with all four legs, and your leg sets are complete.

Put one leg set inside the other and line up the rivet holes. Slip a rivet part way into each side of the stool, place a washer between them, and slide the rivet the rest of the way through as in Fig 16. The stool should work easily, with the washer separating

the leg set enough to keep the legs from rubbing as the stool is opened and closed. (Fig. 17) Set the stool up and use a loop of tied string to keep the legs in what will be their usual position when the stool is opened. This allows you to test the stool several times before peening the rivets over, and makes it easier to measure the length needed for the seat material.

Finally, slip a washer over the end of each rivet and peen it in place. I've already discussed riveting in the tools and techniques section of Chapter 2, so I won't repeat the procedure here.

## Stitching it up

The last part of the project is to make the seat, which involves a couple decisions on your part. The fabric seats on these stools were attached in one of two ways. Both methods appear in surviving samples as well as in the photographic record, so both are perfectly correct. You can see a comparison of the two in Fig. 18.

The first way involves tacking the seat onto the inner edges of the seat braces, wrapping the fabric down, around the outside edge, and then over the tops of the braces. Done this way, weight is spread out over all four surfaces of the seat braces, making for a stronger seat and less stress on the tacks. In this method, because the seat must pass through the inside of the inner leg set, it can't be any wider than 10½". In the second method, the seat is tacked onto the outer edges of the seat braces and simply wrapped over the top. There will be more stress on the tacks this way, as the weight is spread across only two surfaces of the brace. However, since the seat material never passes through the center of the leg sets, this method allows for a wider seat, up to the full 15" width of the seat braces. The extra fabric width allows for a few more tacks, as well.

For the inner-tacking method with a 10½"-wide seat, the fabric should measure 22" or 23" long. If you opt for a 15"-wide seat tacked onto the outer edge, the fabric should be 18" to 19" long.

So there's your decision: a wider, more comfortable seat with a bit less strength, or a slightly narrower seat that's stronger.

I've used 100%-cotton tapestry fabric for the seat, which I highly recommend due to its frequent appearance in surviving samples and the

## SOME THOUGHTS ON STOOL AUTHENTICITY

It's one thing to make sure that a Civil War reproduction is accurate and period-correct, but it also has to be used correctly. The stool in this project is patterned after an original, so I know it's correct. It would be completely inauthentic, however, if it were used by a private in a campaign scenario. When on campaign, marches of 20 miles a day and more weren't unusual, and the common foot soldier carried only what he absolutely needed to sustain him. Officers would have had all kinds of comforts carried on wagons, but the only seat a foot soldier would have had was the seat of his pants.

The camp stool in this project is highly authentic, but sometimes the most authentic stool is none at all.

photographic record. Tapestry fabric isn't long lasting when used by itself as seat material, and it has a tendency to stretch a lot, so it should be backed up with a layer of another material such as cotton duck (canvas).

To make a tapestry seat, cut a piece of tapestry and a piece of heavy cotton duck to the size of the seat you want, plus ½" on each side. Lay the two pieces together—the "good" side of the tapestry facing in—and stitch ½" in down both sides to create a fabric tube. Turn the seat right side out so the good side of the tapestry is now showing. Run a double row of stitching across each end.

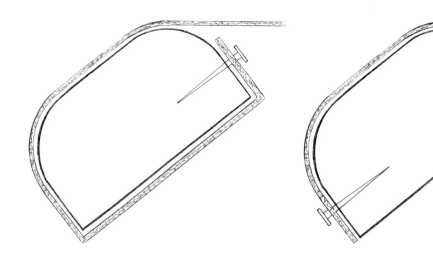

*Figure 18*

For a canvas seat, I recommend making the seat in a doubled layer just as with the tapestry version for the most strength possible, but some surviving samples show that canvas was often done in a single layer. (These may have been simple field repairs.) For a single-layer canvas seat, cut your fabric to the desired seat size, plus 1" on each side. Fold the raw edges over about ¼", then fold over a second time about ½" to ¾". Run a row of stitching near the inside edge of the fold. Finally, run a double row of stitching across each end of the seat.

Attach the seat with ⅝" to ¾" steel, brass or copper tacks as in Fig. 19, placing the tacks an inch or less apart.

## Variations

I chose walnut for this stool for two reasons: It's one of my favorite woods, and the stool I saw in the museum was walnut. You may have noticed in the photos that the stool's rungs looked lighter than the walnut. Good eye; they're oak. The museum sample I saw clearly had oak rungs, although I'm not sure that was done intentionally for the handsome contrast between the two woods; more likely the stool had been repaired to replace broken rungs and available oak doweling was used in place of the original walnut. Either way, I liked it so I used oak. You may wish to make yours entirely of walnut.

*Figure 19*

However, you can use any hardwood you like. For darker woods like walnut and cherry, a simple oil finish will darken the wood and bring out the grain pattern. Lighter woods like oak, hickory or ash may be stained or left natural. For any wood, a coat of shellac would also have been correct to the period for a stool of this type.

Alter the curve of the legs as you wish. Also, when you assemble the seat as you did back in Fig. 16, you can reverse the leg sets so the curve goes the opposite direction if you like.

Another way to attach the seat is to cut the seat fabric about 5" longer, then fold over and stitch the ends to form something like a tube. Unscrew the seat braces and slip this tube over the braces on each side of the stool, then screw the braces back into place. No tacks are needed in this method, but the seat must be narrow enough to fit inside the inner leg set.

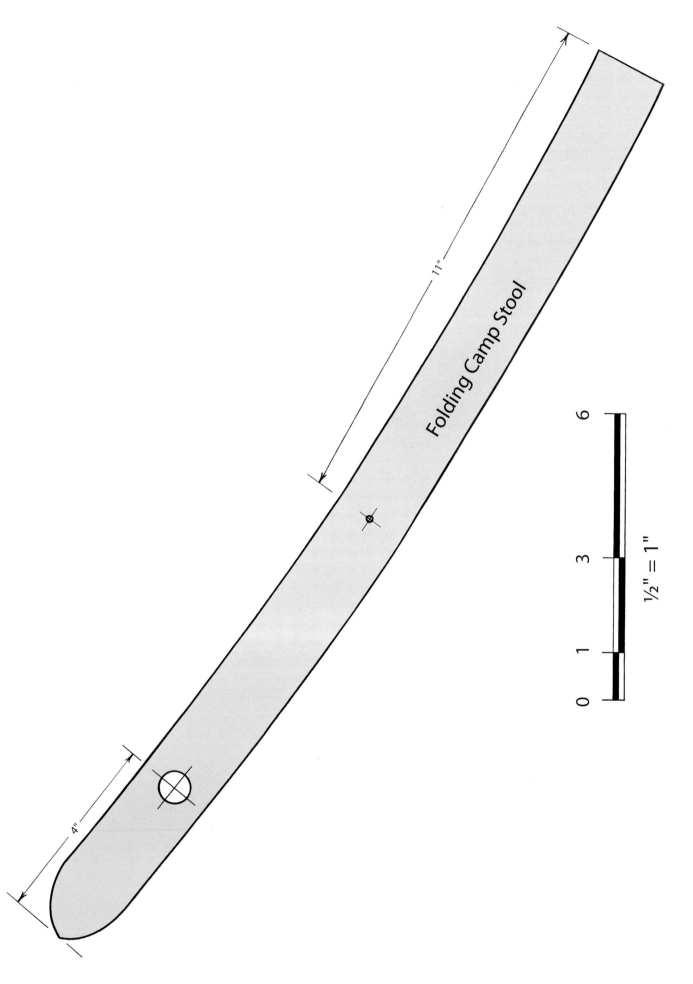

Folding Camp Stool

11"

4"

0   1   3   6

½" = 1"

# Chapter 9:
# LT. KELLY'S CAMP CHAIR

When I discovered the photo of this chair in the Library of Congress archives, I thought it was perfect to include here. The camp scene with four officers showed good detail, and the chair that caught my eye was a handsome one. Further, the photo description listed the officers' names and ranks, so I could positively identify the young lieutenant in the chair.

At the time, however, I didn't realize the chair had armrests. Lt. Kelly's left hand is in his lap, and it looked to me like the armrest on his right belonged to the other officer's chair. But when I enlarged the photo for a closer look, I noticed a broken hinge near Kelly's left elbow and assumed the chair once had armrests, but I was clueless as to what they might have looked like. On a hunch, I searched the other officers' names and two more photos of the same scene popped up. Each photo was from a slightly different angle and gave a better look at details. More importantly, the officers shuffled their positions for each shot, and it became suddenly clear that what I thought was an armrest on the other chair was, in fact, on Kelly's. I now had three photos of the same chair, numerous details and a good look at the armrest. Since Kelly was in the chair in two of the three photos, I named the project after him.

The photographic record of the war shows that sling chairs of this type were very popular with officers. Most were of a simpler design with straight

LIBRARY OF CONGRESS

*Lt. Kelly* (right) *relaxes in a comfortable camp chair at Army of the Potomac headquarters, Culpeper, Va., in September of 1863.*

*Marvin Miracle of Carlin's Battery, 1st W.Va. Light Artillery, tries out this chapter's reproduction of Lt. Kelly's Camp Chair.*

## *Cut List*
## LT. KELLY'S CAMP CHAIR

Overall Dimensions: 22½" wide, standing approximately 49" high

| Name | Qty. | Wood | Dimensions |
|---|---|---|---|
| Long Legs/Back | 2 | Oak | 1¼" x 1¼" x 52" |
| Short Legs/Seat | 2 | Oak | 1¼" x 1¼" x 35" |
| Headrest Stretcher | 1 | Oak | 1" x 3¾" x 20" (a) |
| Seat Stretcher | 1 | Oak | 1" x 3" x 17⅜" (a) |
| Armrests | 2 | Oak | 1¼" x 1¼" x 14¼" (b) |
| Armrest Supports | 2 | Oak | 1¼" x 1¼" x 9¼" |
| Leg Bracers | 2 | Oak | ¾" x 1¼" x 24" |
| Upper Seat Tacking Rail | 1 | Oak | 1" x 1" x 20" |
| Lower Seat Tacking Rail | 1 | Oak | 1" x 1" x 17⅜" |

**Notes:**

(a) Length shown is shoulder-to-shoulder distance and does not include tenons.
   Be sure to include sufficient overall length of workpiece to cut tenons.
(b) Cut armrest from stock 2¼" wide to accommodate width of rounded end.

*See drawings on pages 104 and 105. Patterns on pages 106 and 107.*

leg components, basic joinery, and no armrests. Lt. Kelly's chair is fancier and the product of a well-equipped shop; from its gently curved leg components to the mortise-and-tenon joinery in the headrest and seat stretchers, it was certainly brought into the field from someone's home. Clearly, the chair has been heavily used—one armrest missing, the other appears to be leaning and coming loose, the finish is scratched and dull.

In this project, we'll return Kelly's chair to like-new condition and replace the missing armrest. I'll even give you the option of making it without armrests for an easier-to-make project.

## Getting started

In the enlarged views, the chair is clearly made of oak, with the main components measuring 1¼" x 1¼" square. This is an educated guess, of course, but comparing the chair to other objects in the photos, plus what would be needed for strength, I'm betting I hit it on the nose. Based on that measurement, the headrest and seat stretcher would be 1" thick.

This means you'll need a source of oak of at least 1¼" thick. You won't find that at your local home center, so visit a lumber supplier. Even at a lumber dealer you may be limited to sizes in ½" or even 1" increments, and if so you'll have to buy the next thicker size. You might be able to have them mill thicker lumber down to 1¼" for you; if you own a planer you can mill it yourself.

Lay out the patterns for the leg components on your 1¼" stock as in Fig. 1. Note that this is one big, heavy piece of wood, so if you have a wide piece of lumber like I have lay out the patterns first, then cut the piece in two to make it more manageable (Fig 2).

Cut out the components using the pattern lines as a guide. Both a bandsaw and jigsaw work well for this (Figs. 3 & 4). Note in Fig. 3 how I've trimmed some waste away first before cutting out the patterns; this eliminates a lot of extra weight, making the workpiece easier to maneuver.

Figure 1

Figure 2

Figure 3

Figure 4

No matter how carefully you draw the patterns and cut them, it's very difficult turning out exact pairs in these sizes. So, when you cut out the components don't cut right to the line. In Fig. 5 you

Figure 5

Figure 7

Figure 6

can see I've left a slight bit of waste around each component. This will allow us to fine-tune the parts into exact pairs.

To do this, attach each pair of components together. Using the patterns as a guide, transfer the locations of the mortises and main rivet pivoting point to the components. Clamp the pieces together and drill a pilot hole through the mortise and rivet locations as in Fig. 6, then drive screws to hold the components together into a single workpiece. (These areas will be cut and drilled later, so the screws won't leave damage.) Now, using a sander or hand plane, refine the components down to the pattern lines you drew (Fig. 7).

Remove the screw from the rivet location, but leave the one in the mortise for now. With the legs still attached in pairs, drill a ¼" hole at the rivet location in each pair. *Do not* drill the rivet holes for the armrests at this time. Remove the remaining

screw at the mortise location, and you now have identical leg pairs.

## Construct the leg sets

The headrest stretcher and the seat stretcher attach to the legs with mortise-and-tenon joinery, among the strongest woodworking joints. From the original photos, we can see that these are through mortises, in that the ends of the tenons extend all the way through the legs.

As with the Bucksaw Project, we'll follow the general rule of making the tenons about a third the thickness of the workpieces. Both stretchers are 1" thick, but a third of 1" is ⅓", an odd measurement for woodworking joinery, so we'll round that up to ⅜".

Mark your mortises as indicated on the pattern; the seat mortise is ⅜" x 2⅜", while the headrest mortise is ⅜" x 3". In Figs. 8 and 9, I'm cutting the mortise on one of the long legs using a benchtop mortiser with a ⅜" bit, but you can also cut them with a drill and chisel as described in the Bucksaw Project chapter. If you use a mortising machine, it's imperative that you keep the workpiece level while cutting; note how I've knocked together a temporary support for the leg to keep it level.

With all four mortises done, cut the tenons on the ends of the headrest and seat stretchers to fit the mortises. The overall length of the stretchers includes the tenons on each end, but it's the distance between the shoulders of the tenons that determines

Figure 8

Figure 9

Figure 10

Figure 11

how far apart the leg sets are. The shoulders of the tenons on the headrest stretcher are 20" apart; for the seat stretcher 17⅜". When cutting out these workpieces, you'll need to add a minimum of 1¼" to each side for the tenons. However, it's best to add a bit more, make the tenon longer than needed, and then trim it to length later. This way you don't risk making tenons that are too short, and once trimmed you'll have through tenons that are perfectly flush.

Let's add 1½" to each end of the stretchers to give us a good margin. With that in mind, the overall length of the headrest stretcher will be 23"; the seat stretcher will be 20⅜". Getting a tenon exactly right to fit a mortise can be tricky, so when you cut the stretcher workpieces from 1" stock, cut an extra practice piece of the same stock. Set the real workpieces aside for a moment while we work with the practice piece.

Tenons can be cut on a router table as we did with the Bucksaw, but we'll use the tablesaw with a dado blade set to cut them for this project. Adjust the height of your dado blade to give you a tenon of the correct thickness—to get a ⅜" tenon in 1" stock, set the height at 5⁄16". Cut a test tenon by passing the practice workpiece over the dado blade on each side, and test-fit it into your mortise. If the tenon is too thin, lower the blade on your dado set; if it's too thick, raise it. Make adjustments in tiny increments; it's easy to go past the correct height. Cut the end of the test piece off squarely and try again as many times as you need to (Fig. 10). When your practice tenon is the right thickness, the saw is set perfectly to cut the tenons on the real stretchers. Now grab those two stretcher workpieces you cut earlier, measure in 1½" from each end to mark the tenon shoulders. (Double check that the measurements between your marks are 20" and 17⅜".) Run the stretchers in multiple passes over the dado blade to cut all four sides, as in Fig. 11.

# CSI: Culpeper

Re-creating furniture from photographs is one of the biggest challenges in woodworking, and often turns into a detective story. Fortunately, for Lt. Kelly's Camp Chair I had three photos from his campsite in Culpeper, Va., to work with, each taken a few minutes apart and from slightly different angles.

Some details that were clear in one photo couldn't be seen in others, and vice-versa. For example, the close-up in Fig. 1 gave a great look at those pegged mortise-and-tenon joints when another officer was in the chair. Likewise, the enlarged portion from the second photo shown in Fig. 2 showed the broken hinge where the missing armrest had been, plus good detail

and practical to use, yet it still had to form a parallelogram in order to fold correctly. As before I tried several test arrangements with foam board first, followed by a mock-up in some scrap wood. For the mock-up I actually mounted hinges and installed the rivets to test the folding action. (Since I was just testing the folding movement, there was no need to make the legs full-length.) In Fig. 5 the armrest in the open position looked good and solid, but the real test was next. The result, in Fig. 6 showed that I had gotten it exactly right.

Case solved! All that was left now was to transfer all my templates and mock-ups to the real workpieces and start woodworking.

Fig. 1

Fig. 2

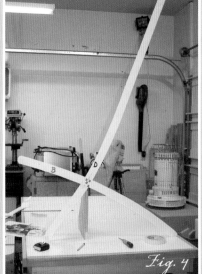

Fig. 4

of the seat bracers and their placement, and the through mortise on the front of the seat. And the zoomed-in detail in Fig. 3 gave me an idea of the armrest shape, as well as the hinge placement underneath.

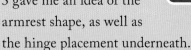

Fig. 3

Putting all these clues together, the next step in re-creating the chair was to get the short and long legs correct. I started by simply sketching on a notepad till I had the right shapes and lengths, then followed that with a foam board cutout, using trial and error to get the pivot point correct, as in Fig. 4.

After that was the armrest, the hardest part of this project: The armrest had to be comfortable

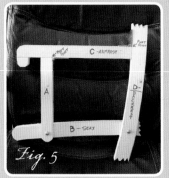

Fig. 5

Fig. 6

*Figure 12*

*Figure 13*

Now, you've probably noticed that while the tenon on the seat stretcher is a perfect fit, the tenon on the headrest stretcher is just a little too long for the mortise you cut for it earlier. However, the headrest will be curved at the top, which would have exposed the top of the mortise. For that reason make the mortise ⅛" shorter on top, which will keep it hidden once the headrest is curved. To accommodate this, shorten the tenon on the top of the headrest stretcher by raising the dado blade to ⁷⁄₁₆" and make another pass on that side as in Fig. 12.

Draw a curve on the top edge of the headrest stretcher making sure the ends of the curve are at least ⅛" above the tenon, and cut out the curve with a bandsaw, scrollsaw or jigsaw. With a roundover bit, round the top curve of the headrest and the front edge of the seat. This is the same process I described for the Camp Stool in the previous chapter, so I won't repeat it here.

The seat material attaches to the headrest and seat stretchers using a tacking rail. We won't attach the seat for a while, but it's easier to prepare the tacking rails now before the chair is assembled. Put each stretcher in a vise, rounded edge down, and clamp the tacking rail in place on the flat edge. Starting about an inch from each end, drill five evenly spaced countersunk pilot holes through the rail and into the stretchers (Fig. 13). Go ahead and drive a #10 x 1¾" screw into each hole to thread it, then back the screw out. You can use brass screws if you prefer, but stronger plain-steel screws are a better choice.

*Figure 14*

Apply glue to the tenon and inside the leg set mortises, and clamp the stretchers in place (Fig. 14). Be sure to orient the stretchers the correct way: Flat edges face the long direction of the legs.

Close examination of the original photos shows that the mortise-and-tenon joints in Kelly's chair—already very strong—were further strengthened with pegs. While the leg sets are still clamped up, drill a pair of ⅜" holes through the face of each leg, right through the tenon, and out the other side.

*Step 1*

*Step 2*

*Step 3*

*Figure 15*

(Place a piece of scrap underneath so the drill bit doesn't tear out the wood on the underside of the stretcher.) Apply glue into each hole and drive in a length of ⅜" oak dowel. When the glue has dried, cut off the excess dowel and sand flush. This three-step process is shown in Fig. 15.

When the glue in the mortise-and-tenon joints has dried completely, trim and sand the tenons flush.

## Chair assembly

As with the Camp Stool, one leg set fits inside the other and are riveted on each side. Temporarily clamp a piece of scrap across the inner leg set (this is the shorter set that forms the seat) near the rivet hole to support it, then place the inner leg set inside the outer one. For each side, slide a rivet in from the outside, separated by a washer between the two sets. Finally, put a washer over the end of the rivets and peen them in place as in Fig. 16. I've already discussed riveting in the tools and techniques section of Chapter 2, so I won't repeat it here.

So, what's this chair going to look like? You're about to find out. Right now, the leg bracers that hold the chair rigidly in an upright position aren't yet attached, so you'll need some help keeping the chair up while you secure them. The easiest way to do this is to clamp two lengths of wood to a workbench or assembly table, and set the chair up inside them. To help locate the leg bracers, place

these two wood pieces exactly 26⅜" apart; they'll hold the chair in the exact orientation to place the bracers accurately (Fig. 17).

Cut the leg bracers to size, rounding the ends as shown in Fig. 18. Apply a bit of glue to the mounting spots on the legs and clamp the bracers in place. When dry, drill countersunk pilot holes in the ends of each bracer and drive in a #10 x 1½" screw (Fig. 19). Note in this photo that before gluing and clamping the bracers in place that I've cut a small angled notch in them for the legs to rest in, similar to the one for the winding paddle on the Bucksaw Project. This adds a bit of additional snugness for supporting the legs, but is entirely optional.

At this point you can consider your chair complete if you'd like. Many chairs of this type did not include armrests—remember, I originally thought Lt. Kelly's chair didn't have any—and your

*Figure 16*

Figure 17

Figure 18

Figure 19

Figure 20

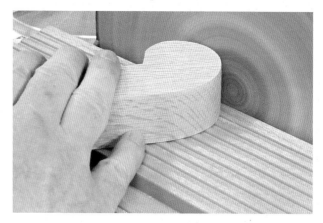

Figure 21

If you'd prefer an armless chair, jump ahead to the "Finishing up" section.

## Making the armrests

As stated above, making the armrests is a bit tricky, so it's a good idea to save drilling the armrest rivet hole and cutting the hinge mortises on the chair for last. This way, if the process of making the armrests doesn't go well you can abandon them with no harm done to the chair itself.

Start the armrests by cutting out the components. A disk sander works well to smooth the rounded ends of the armrests and supports (Fig. 21). Drill a ¼" rivet hole in each armrest support as indicated on the pattern (page 106).

chair is perfectly authentic without them. Adding armrests is a bit complicated, and involves some unusual mortising and getting a lot of angles to work right. Further, without armrests the chair folds flat, as in Fig. 20. With armrests attached it won't fold completely flat, much like regular folding lawn chairs.

*Figure 22*

*Figure 23*

*Figure 24*

The next step is to cut mortises for the hinges. The exact size of your mortise may vary depending on the hinges you get, but the pivot point remains the same: 8½" from the square end of the armrest. Measure 8½" from the end and mark a line. Lay the hinge on the armrest with the barrel centered on your line and trace its outline. With a freshly sharpened chisel, carefully cut out the hinge mortise to the exact thickness of the hinge leaf—check this frequently as you chisel (Fig. 22). Depending on your hinges, you may also need to cut a relief for the hinge barrel to allow the hinge to lie flat in the mortise. A round file works well for this, as in Fig. 23.

Set the hinge in the finished mortise and hold the armrest support up to it, then trace the other leaf of the hinge on the armrest support. Mortise this the same way, keeping in mind that you may need to use the round file again to cut a relief for

the hinge barrel on the end of the armrest support right at the pivot point.

When both mortises are cut, you should be able to place the armrest support against the armrest and hold the hinge in place to check for fit. If all looks good, drill pilot holes and screw the hinge in place. When finished, the armrest assembly should fold smoothly; in the open position (when the armrest and support make a right angle), the end of the support should rest firmly against the underside of the armrest itself.

At this point, you have one last hinge mortise to cut on the assembly, located on top of the armrest where it meets the back of the chair. Because the pivot point for this hinge is at the very end of the armrest, this is cut the same way as the one you did for the top of the armrest support. Drill pilot holes and screw the hinge in place.

To attach the armrest assembly, first clamp it in the open, right-angle position. Now hold it against the side of the chair so the end of the armrest is perfectly perpendicular to the upper portion of the chair as in Fig. 24. Adjust as needed so the rivet hole falls as close to the center of the seat as you can get it. This is the position the armrest will be in when the chair is set up. Now mark the top of the hinge for the mortise you'll cut in the chair itself.

Fold up the chair and lay it flat; because of the curve, you'll need to place a support underneath so it doesn't rock. Now, use an extra hinge to lay out

*Figure 25*

the mortise and cut it as you did the one on the underside of the armrest in Figs. 22 and 23. Note that this pivot point and hinge mortise is a mirror image of the one underneath the armrest. Cut the mortise as before, drill pilot holes, and screw the hinge in place. With the chair still lying flat, unfold it to the open position. You may need to clamp it to the table to keep it open. Hold the open armrest firmly against the side of the chair, then use the hole in the armrest support as a guide to drill through the chair seat as in Fig. 25. Your ¼" drill bit may not go all the way through the combined 2½" thickness of the support and chair seat (which is why I'm not worried about drilling through my finger in the photo). Go as far as you can, retract the drill, drop the armrest out of the way, then finish the hole in the seat.

Slip in a rivet (don't forget a washer between the armrest support and seat), add a washer to the inside, peen over the rivet, and the armrest is attached. Now, repeat with the other side of the chair.

## Finishing up

Kelly's chair looks dark in the photos and was likely stained, which would have been the practice for a piece of shop-made furniture of this quality. The process of making today's stains has changed little since the 19th century, so I have no qualms recommending a modern walnut-colored stain. You can mix up your own stain from scratch if you want (hundreds of stain "recipes" are available online that use pigment, BLO and mineral spirits), but an oil-based stain you can get in a can contains the same ingredients and the results are identical. Apply the stain evenly, allow it to penetrate for a few minutes, then wipe off the excess.

Allow the stain to dry for the length of time recommended on the label, usually 12 to 24 hours. When the stain is dry, give the chair a few coats of shellac. You can use ready-made shellac available in a can, or mix up your own the old-fashioned way; the results will be the same and both are period-correct. I like the look of amber shellac on walnut-stained oak—it gives the wood a warm, mellow look, but you can use a clear shellac if you prefer. For authenticity, avoid all modern varnishes such as polyurethane.

All that's left now is making the seat. I'm betting Kelly's chair originally had a tapestry seat like the one on the Camp Stool in the last chapter, but the photos clearly show a canvas seat so that's what I've made here.

You'll need a few yards of heavy, 100% cotton duck (canvas). Cut a piece 52" long and 23" wide. Because the seat leg set is 2⅝" narrower than the back leg set, you'll need to taper the canvas seat by that much for a proper fit at the bottom. Make a mark 1⁵⁄₁₆" from each corner at the bottom, then use a pencil to draw a straight line from your marks to the upper corners. Cut along the lines to get the tapered canvas.

Time for some sewing and ironing. Fold over each long edge ½" and iron flat. Now fold the same edges over 1" and iron again. (If you've followed the math here, you'll note that this folding cuts the width of the seat by 1½" on each side, making the seat now 20" wide at the top and 17⅜" at the bottom—the exact width of the headrest and seat stretchers.) Run a row of stitching along the inside fold. Now fold each end over ½" and iron flat, followed by a row of stitching to secure the fold.

A sewing machine is fine and period-correct for this, as long as you use a plain, straight stitch and cotton thread. Feel free to sew by hand, however.

Attach each end of the seat to the tacking rails by driving some ⅝" to ¾" steel, brass or copper tacks through that ½" fold on the ends. The tacks should be about an inch or so apart. Be sure you get the orientation of the seat correct so that the tacks are on the underside of the tacking rail, and the canvas goes in between the tacking rail and the seat and headrest stretchers. Hold the tacking rails in place, and drive five #10 x 1¾" screws to hold the rail in place as in Fig. 26. This makes for a strong seat mounting: The tacks hold the canvas to the rail, which in turn clamps the canvas to the stretchers. Note that in this photo that I have not yet stained and finished the chair.

## Variations

I chose oak for this chair to match Kelly's original, but hickory and ash would also be good choices. Do not make this chair with softwood; that might be OK for a chair with perfectly straight components, but the curved legs of this chair would not be strong enough at these dimensions in softwood.

My choice of a canvas seat matched the chair in the photo, but by all means consider a tapestry seat as that is undoubtedly what the chairmaker used when he first crafted the chair.

As stated earlier, feel free to make this chair without armrests; armless chairs of this type were very common. Of course, if you really want to make this chair a replica of Lt. Kelly's original, make it with one armrest missing.

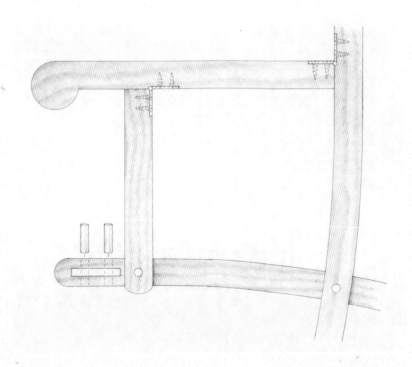

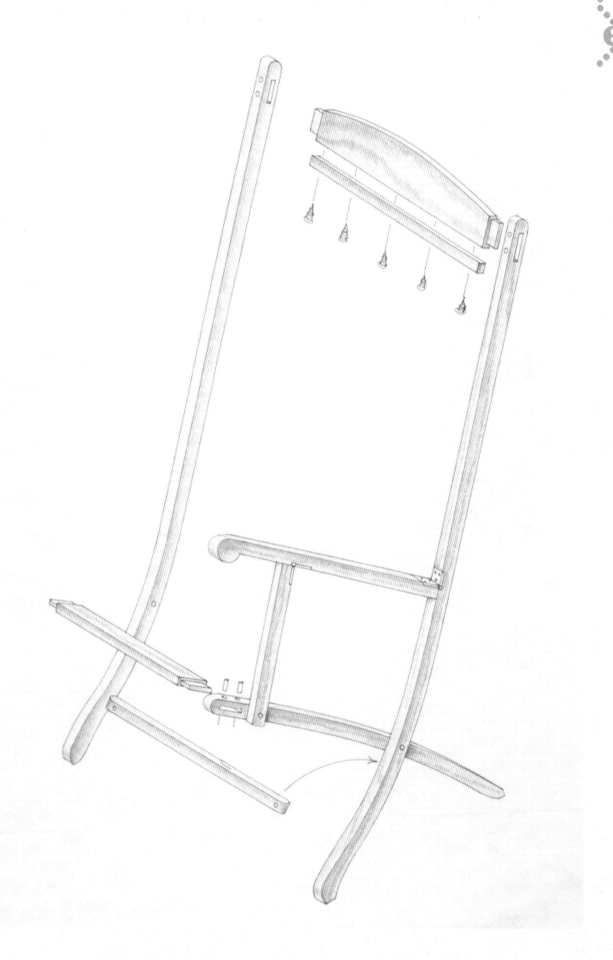

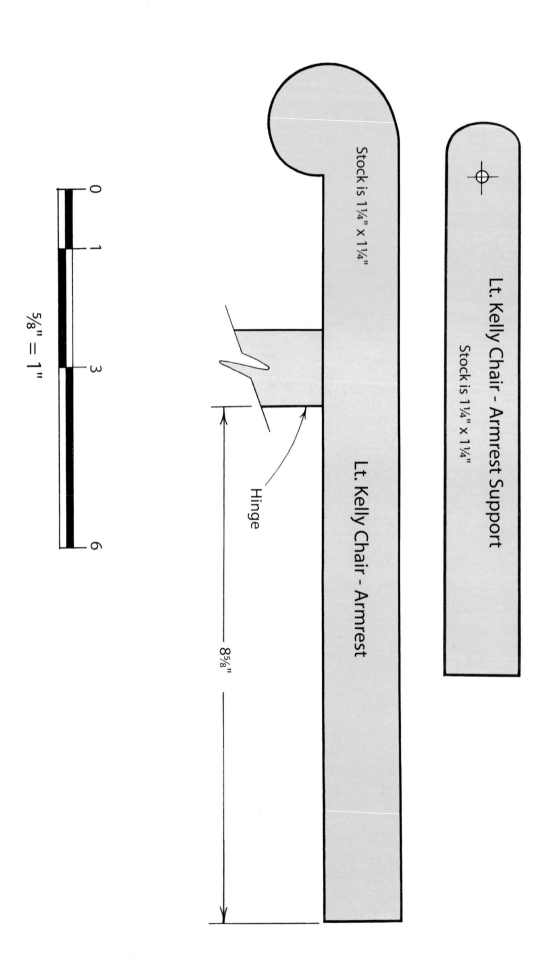

Stock is 1¼" x 1¼"

Lt. Kelly Chair - Armrest Support

Stock is 1¼" x 1¼"

Hinge

Lt. Kelly Chair - Armrest

8⅝"

⅝" = 1"

0
1
3
6

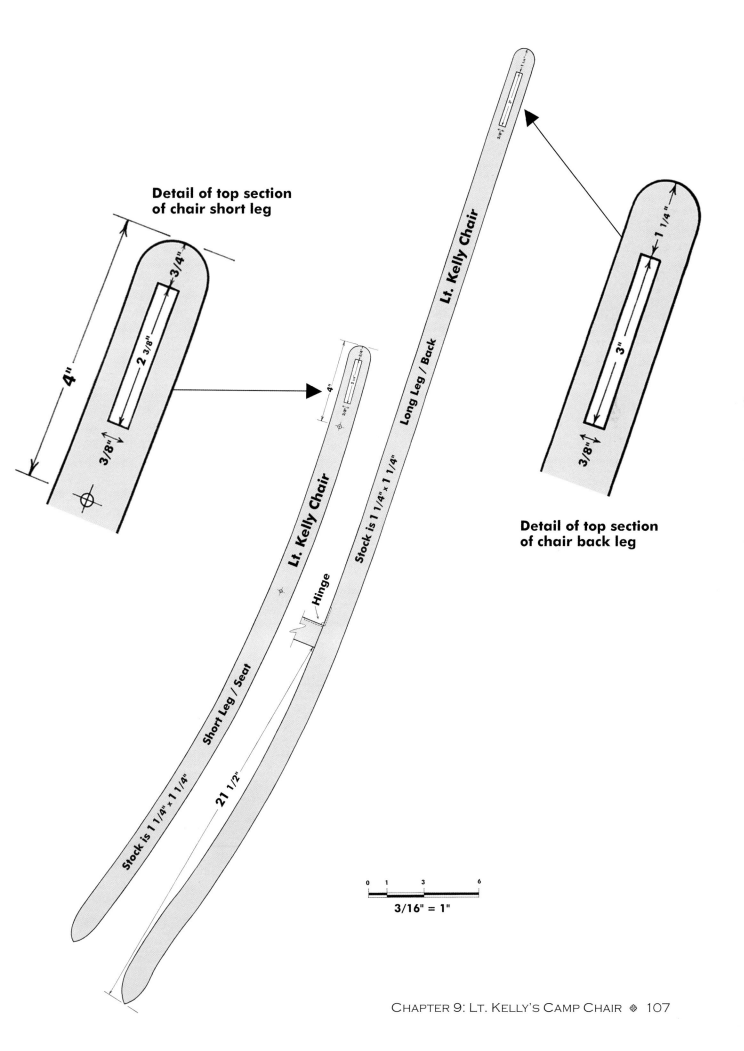

**Detail of top section
of chair short leg**

4"

2 3/8"

3/4"

3/8"

**Detail of top section
of chair back leg**

1 1/4"

3"

3/8"

**Lt. Kelly Chair**

**Long Leg / Back**

**Stock is 1 1/4" x 1 1/4"**

4"

2 1/4"

3/4"

3/8"

Hinge

**Lt. Kelly Chair**

**Short Leg / Seat**

**Stock is 1 1/4" x 1 1/4"**

21 1/2"

0   1   3   6
3/16" = 1"

*Field desks were used on any*
*available flat surface, but teaming*
*one with the Folding Camp Table*
*from Chapter 6 makes an especially*
*good match.*

# Chapter 10:
# OFFICER'S FIELD DESK

When we think of a desk today, we think of a big expansive work surface with lots of drawers underneath. Those desks existed in the 19th century, but back then when most people thought of a desk they envisioned a small, vertical cabinet with a drop-down front. Inside were several small cubbyholes, a few vertical or horizontal slots for papers or ledgers, and maybe a drawer or two. Far more common than their large modern counterparts, these desks were meant to be set on tables; the drop-down front was the writing surface.

Variables for these desks were many, with sizes and internal designs all over the board. Some were almost entirely cubbyholes and nothing else, while others contained mostly drawers. Some were made of exquisite hardwoods featuring exotic inlays, while others were simplicity itself. Some were much taller than they were wide, others just the opposite. After many years studying the Civil War and after researching every surviving desk I could find in preparation for the project presented here, I think I've seen no fewer than a hundred examples. Not once did I see two desks that were the same.

©2009 WILL DUNNIWAY & COMPANY

*Reenactor Chris Hoshaw, Union Brigade Commander with the National Civil War Assocation, tends to regimental business at a reproduction of a typical field desk of the period.*

# OFFICER'S FIELD DESK

Overall Dimensions: 11¼" x 17⅝" x 27¼"

| Name | Qty. | Wood | Dimensions |
|---|---|---|---|
| CARCASE: | | | |
| Back | 1 | SPF | ⅝" x 17" x 26" (a) |
| Top/Bottom | 2 | SPF | ⅝" x 9¾" x 26" (a) |
| Ends | 2 | SPF | 1" x 9¾" x 15¾" (a) |
| Door Mounting Strip | 1 | SPF | ⅝" x 1⅜" x 26" |
| Formal Top | 1 | SPF | ⅝" x 17⅝" x 27¼" |
| CENTER MODULE: | | | |
| Sides | 2 | SPF | ½" x 9¼" x 15¾" |
| Shelves | 2 | SPF | ½" x 8" x 9¼" |
| Dividers | 2 | SPF | ½" x 7" x 8¾" |
| DIVIDERS: | | | |
| Tall Dividers | 3 | SPF | ½" x 9¼" x 15¾" |
| DRAWER: | | | |
| Sides | 2 | SPF | ½" x 3⁵⁄₁₆" x 9" |
| Front/Back | 2 | SPF | ½" x 3⁵⁄₁₆" x 8" |
| Bottom | 1 | Walnut | ⅛" x 7½" x 8⅞" (b) |
| SHELF STACK: | | | |
| Sides | 8 | SPF | ⅜" x 3½" x 8½" |
| Shelves | 3 | SPF | ½" x 7⅜" x 8½" |
| DOOR: | | | |
| Frame Stiles | 2 | SPF | ⅝" x 2½" x 15⅝" |
| Frame Rails | 2 | SPF | ⅝" x 2½" x 21" (c) |
| Panel | 1 | SPF | ¼" x 11⅛" x 21½" |

**Notes:**

(a) These components are the same as those used in the Hardtack Crate Project.

(b) I used walnut simply because I had it; you can use any wood, although hardwood is recommended for strength.

(c) Listed length of Frame Rails does not include tenon.

*See drawings on pages 124 and 125*

These desks were perfect for officers during the Civil War—light, utilitarian, customizable and eminently portable. As a result of their use by the military in the 19ᵗʰ century, they took on the moniker of "field desk," and it's possible today to find numerous examples for sale in antique stores and online auction sites that, in spite of the fact they never saw duty in the field, are still described by that name.

## Types of field desks

I group field desks into three main categories.

Some men who used desks of this type before the war took them along when they became officers and, as such, they were never really intended for field use at all. These desks were often among the nicest and most elegantly crafted, and were usually considerably larger than the average field desk. One such desk belonged to General Thomas J. "Stonewall" Jackson (see sidebar). The desk he used in the field was actually a schoolmaster's desk, the same one he used while teaching at the Virginia Military Institute when the war broke out. Tall and attractive with dovetailed construction and a hinged top for additional storage, it was the perfect example of a finely crafted desk made by an expert cabinetmaker.

Similar to the Jackson desk with regards construction details were the ones officers commissioned for themselves during the war, either in their hometowns or at cabinet shops near where they might have been stationed for lengthy periods of time. Although usually much smaller than Jackson's desk, these desks also employed fine joinery techniques, and were made with locally available hardwoods like walnut, oak, maple and cherry.

The second type of field desk was often a hurried, makeshift affair constructed in the field. Made with whatever wood was available—and sometimes wood not in the best shape, at that—these desks were cobbled together and usually extremely basic. Often, they were made quickly by someone with few woodworking skills or tools, and were just wooden boxes with a hinged door, and some shelves and cubbyholes inside. It wasn't unusual that existing boxes or crates were used, with hinges appropriated from a nearby house. Not pretty, but these desks got the job done.

Then there were the field desks that fell in the middle of these other two extremes. Although soldier-made in the field, the maker was often someone who was a skilled carpenter or cabinetmaker in civilian life. Usually, these desks were made when the army stayed in one spot for a while, near towns with ready access to tools and materials. In other cases, the regiment may have had one or even several skilled craftsmen among their numbers, and may have carried a generous supply of woodworking tools. These desks still would have been made with whatever wood was available, and so you'd find desks made of SPF materials a bit more frequently than hardwoods. And you'd find quite a few that were made from existing boxes, expertly adapted to their new use. These desks weren't fancy like those from working cabinet shops, but they were well made, versatile and often quite attractive.

It's this third type of desk you'll be making for this project.

# DESK JOB

Joe Cress of Abingdon, Va., has been a woodworker for most of his life. He used to make a good living building hundreds upon hundreds of laminated industrial cabinets a year, but he hated every minute of it.

"I was very good at laminate work, but you're basically just spitting that stuff out," he recalls. "The only thing good about working like that is the money."

*Stonewall Jackson's field desk is the flagship item in Cress' furniture line.*

*Joe Cress with his reproduction of J.E.B. Stuart's field desk.*

A Civil War buff, Cress toured the museum at the Virginia Military Institute while on an estimating trip about 15 years ago. When he saw Stonewall Jackson's field desk and got a close look at the craftsmanship of the desk, he knew he had to make one. Working closely with Lt. Col. Keith Gibson, director of the museum, he acquired an exclusive license to make reproductions of the desk. Good-bye, laminated cabinets; hello, Civil War furniture. Almost overnight, Cress' life changed for good—his company, Logan Creek Designs, was born.

Today, in addition to Jackson's desk, Cress also makes exacting reproductions of field desks belonging to J.E.B. Stuart and Robert E. Lee, as well as several other furniture items related to the Civil War. Cress works at a leisurely pace, turning out 30 to 35 pieces a year from his line, plus occasional commissions for longtime customers from his cabinet-shop days. When he first started Logan Creek, he did everything he could to keep a strict schedule because that's what he was used to when building cabinets. But it just didn't fit.

"This is a whole different thing," he says. "I had to slow down. So now I tell people it'll be mid-fall or early spring, something like that. It's not like I'm the 'desk Nazi' saying, 'No desk for you!' It's just that the schedule was killing me, and sometimes I'd be building five of them at a time. So, I decided I wasn't going to make a lot of money in woodworking. The kind of woodworking you have to do to make money, I don't like it. You have to make a million things and just keep going. I made more money in one year during the '80s than I've made in all the years working on this whole project. But I'm a lot happier now."

You can see examples of Cress' work at www.logancreekdesigns.com.

# Desk design

This desk is not based on any single example, but rather on details from several desks. I've designed it so that it uses wood that would be typically available to a skilled carpenter in the field scavenged from a variety of sources, some of which would have been from dismantling other items and repurposing the wood.

Our hypothetical regimental carpenter used a discarded hardtack crate in good shape as his starting point—in an odd coincidence, the crate he found exactly matches the one in Chapter 4—and as a result many of the other components for this desk are based on existing dimensions of that crate. The rest of the wood came from other crates, boxes and discarded items, and he may have even gotten some from a nearby farmhouse. This skilled carpenter would have wanted to impress and please his commanding officer in spite of the materials available to him, so in all cases he would have selected the best he could find, and cleaned it up considerably with a hand plane, scraper and/or sandpaper. The hinges and lock he used could also have come from a nearby home, or perhaps were taken from other broken furniture. (Both armies left a trail of broken, discarded items behind them as they moved.)

This desk design includes one drawer, but is easily adaptable to have a second (or none, for that matter). The shelves on the right side are not attached, and you can slide them out to create a larger space on that side. All joinery in the main carcase consists of butt joints, as that's how the hardtack crate was made. Other parts of the desk are bit fancier: The drop-down front has a tongue-and-grooved frame with a slide-in panel, while the drawer is rabbeted at the corners and has grooves on each of the sides to accept a thin, slide-in bottom panel.

Obviously, I used the hardtack crate I made earlier as the main carcase of this field desk, so I

*Figure 1*

already have a head start. If you haven't done so already, refer to Chapter 4 and use the instructions there to create one. (If you'd prefer not to use the hardtack crate, I'll include thoughts on varying the carcase at the end of this chapter.)

Start by checking the interior measurements of your crate. (Fig. 1) If you made it to the exact dimensions I specified in Chapter 4, your crate should measure 9¾" x 15¾" x 24" on the inside; all of the instructions and component sizes cited in this project are based on those dimensions. So measure carefully—especially the internal height—and adjust your components accordingly.

# Construct the center drawer module

The center module with the drawer and two dividers above is constructed as a single unit, and then slid into place. Cut the sides of the module to size; the length of these pieces will match the interior height of the crate. Since the two shelves and two dividers of the module are in matched pairs, I find it easier to mark them at the same time on two separate workpieces laid side-by-side, as in Fig. 2. This way I can be sure they match exactly. Mark all of your workpieces for identification and

*Figure 2*

*Figure 3*

*Figure 4*

a particularly strong joint, but we'll reinforce it in the next step with nails. (Also, this is not a joint that will receive any amount of stress, so it will be plenty strong enough.) Allow the glue to set a bit, then carefully invert the dividers and drive two or three 1¼" nails through the bottom of the shelf and into the dividers. (Fig. 5)

Place the completed divider shelf on a flat work surface, then sandwich it and the lower shelf between the sides of the center module for a dry assembly to check for fit. If everything looks good, apply glue to the shelf edges and hold the sides of the center module in place to allow the glue to set a bit as I'm doing in Fig. 6. Clamp the center module together as in Fig. 7, and after the glue has dried, reinforce the module by driving three 1¼" nails into the shelves from the outside of the module sides.

*Figure 5*

*Figure 6*

orientation. (Fig. 3) This is always a good practice for any project; whenever possible, do your marking where it will be hidden inside a joint, which saves time later removing markings. I've done the markings here very dark for photographic purposes, however when you do you own marking do it as lightly as possible. Also mark the top shelf for the locations of the dividers, and mark the sides for the locations of both shelves.

Position the two dividers evenly spaced on the top shelf, using glue, as in Fig. 4. This usually isn't

*Figure 7*

*Figure 8*

*Figure 9*

*Figure 10*

*Figure 11*

(Fig. 9) Once you have it correctly positioned—the spaces on the left and right should be about the same size—drive three 1½" nails through the carcase bottom and into the vertical side members of center module. Do the same thing from the top, driving three nails down into each side member, plus two down into each divider. (Fig. 10) Keeping this center module in place won't take much since it's already snug, so no glue is necessary. I used cut headless brads, which are quite thin and nearly invisible once set.

Cut the two tall dividers for the left side of the desk to size, and cut the scalloped shape into the front. (The purpose of the cutout is to make it easier to grasp narrow vertical items from those storage slots.) Test for fit as in Fig. 11. As with the dividers in the center module, these tall dividers are evenly spaced. Once you have them positioned correctly, drive three 1½" nails into them through the top and bottom of the carcase as you did with the center module. Again, no glue necessary.

Test the module for fit and if you have difficulty sliding it into place, use a sanding block on the top and bottom edges to adjust the fit slightly, as in Fig. 8. When adjusted, the completed center module should slide easily, but very snugly, into the carcase.

*Figure 12*

*Figure 13*

# Drawer construction

The drawer for this desk could be made any number of ways: simple butt joints, dovetails, rabbets, tongue-and-groove, mitered. I like rabbet joints a lot. They're strong, simple, easy to make, and can be somewhat forgiving if you don't get them right the first time. The most common field-made joint was the butt joint, of course, but for a skilled carpenter rabbets were probably the joint of choice and perfectly period-correct for a field-made drawer in the hands of someone with the right tools.

Cut your drawer front and back to size first, then cut ½" wide by ⅜"deep rabbets into each end. You can do the rabbets on a tablesaw, but I've elected to do them on the router table as in Fig. 12. As when doing the tenons for the Bucksaw in Chapter 7, note how I'm using a backer board to keep the workpiece square to the fence and prevent tear-out.

Cut a ⅛" groove about ¼" deep on the bottom edges of the front and both sides of the drawer components as in Fig. 13. The groove should be at least ⅛" from the bottom edge of the drawer, so that's where you want to set your tablesaw fence. If you're using a standard blade on your tablesaw, it will make a perfect ⅛"-wide groove.

Now raise the blade to just over ½" and cut the back of the drawer just as you would if you were cutting the same groove (that is, don't move the fence). This will cut a strip off the drawer back and allow you to slip in the bottom panel from the rear when the drawer is completed.

Dry-assemble the drawer for fit, then glue and clamp the drawer. When dry, reinforce each corner with a pair of cut brads. Slide the drawer bottom into place as in Fig. 14, but do not glue in place. Two things you'll notice about the drawer bottom I'm using here. The first is that it's walnut. You can use any type of wood for the drawer bottom, but I happened to have a quantity of ⅛" walnut on hand, so that's what I used. The second thing you'll notice is that I'm using three separate pieces for the drawer bottom. The thin walnut I had was only 3" wide, so I've cut three pieces and am sliding them in separately. Again, that's what I had on hand so that's what I used—just as our hypothetical regimental carpenter would have done. Drawer bottoms of the period were frequently made with multiple pieces, so feel free to do the same, or not; if you prefer a one-piece drawer bottom, that's perfectly fine. Once the bottom is in place, drive a pair of brads through the drawer bottom and up in to the drawer back to hold it in place.

*Figure 14*

*Figure 15*

*Figure 16*

Test-fit the drawer in the desk's center module as in Fig. 15. If the fit is too snug, you can ease it a bit with a sanding block or on a belt sander. Go easy, though; you don't want to sand too much. You can see in this photo where I've added brads to reinforce the corners. Note, too, that when I was testing the drawer for fit how I put a piece of tape on the top. There is no drawer pull yet, and I can pull the tape like a small handle to free the drawer if it's too snug and gets stuck, which can happen. (Don't ask me how I know this.)

As to a drawer pull, there are several options. One of the most common, which I've used here, is to drill a 1" finger hole through the drawer front. Likewise, a carpenter may have cut a small finger notch into the top of the drawer, or tacked on a thin strip of leather to use as drawer pull. I've designed this desk so the center module is recessed by ½", so you could also use a small wooden or brass knob if you'd like. (I recessed the interior components for a different reason, which I'll discuss shortly.) A fancier flush-mounted hinged brass pull of the type often found on nautical cabinetry is another period-correct option.

## Make the "shelf stack"

An assortment of shelves is one of the most common aspects of military field desks. When built by skilled carpenters in a well-equipped cabinet shop, these shelves were usually set into *dadoes*—grooves cut into the carcase sides that allowed them

to slide into place without fasteners. A benefit of this is that the shelves can also slide out to alter the desk capacity. An officer may have wanted to store, say, a small oil lamp inside the desk, so he could simply slide out one shelf to accommodate the lamp.

Field-made desks—especially those made from existing boxes like this one—often omitted this joinery technique and simply nailed the shelves in place as we did the dividers, or nailed thin support strips on the inside that functioned as shelf brackets. A skilled regimental carpenter may have taken a third route and made a shelf stack. This method simulates dadoes, which not only creates a very solid and attractive means of mounting the shelves, but also allows them to be removed at the officer's pleasure.

The concept of stacked shelves is simple: A pair of wooden strips is attached to the sides of the shelf compartment, starting at the bottom, then topped with a shelf. Then two more strips and another shelf, and so on up to the top. I've designed this desk with three equally spaced shelves, but you can alter both the positioning and the number of shelves as you like.

Cut the side strips to width (the desired height of the shelf) as in Fig. 16, then to length as in Fig. 17. I elected to set the shelf compartment back from the center drawer module simply because I liked the look, but you can make your shelves flush with the center if you wish. With the side strips and your shelves all cut to size, now it's simply a matter of gluing and stacking. Start by gluing the two bottom side strips in place, then top with the first shelf as

*Figure 17*

*Figure 19*

*Figure 18*

*Figure 20*

in Fig. 18. Then glue the next two side strips into place, top with the next shelf, and so on. Be careful not to get glue on the edges of the shelves or you won't be able to remove them.

## Door preparation

In some field desks, the door is completely inset inside the carcase; others have the door outside the carcase, attached with hinges to an extension at the bottom of the carcase. If the carcase is made from scratch the bottom component could simply have been made a bit wider, but we'll add a mounting strip to accomplish the task. (Fig. 19)

Adding a separate mounting strip also makes it easier to cut the hinge mortises. Lay the hinges in position and hold them securely in place as you mark the mortise with a sharp pencil or knife, as in Fig. 20. With the strip held firmly in a bench vise, use a sharp chisel to define the ends of the hinge mortise. (Fig. 21) Working carefully, clean out the mortise

*Figure 21*

*Figure 22*

to the correct depth to accept the hinge. (Fig. 22) With both mortises cut, glue and clamp the hinge mounting strip to the bottom front of the carcase.

The front door also needs something at the top of the carcase to register on and to engage the lock. Again, if we had made this carcase from scratch we could have made the top component wider. We could also just add a strip to the top as we did the bottom (and many desks were made exactly that way), but I decided to go a different, slightly more elaborate route and add a formal top to the desk for a couple of reasons. First, of course, it extends the

*Figure 23*

*Figure 24*

*Figure 25*

*Figure 26*

front of the carcase to enclose the top of the door. And because the top also extends on both sides it gives the finished desk some very pleasing lines. The top also hides all the nails we used to mount internal desk components, plus the original nails used to attach that side of the hardtack crate; in fact, the only nails now visible on the exterior of the desk are on the back.

The door on this desk is ⅝" thick, so cut the top to overhang the desk front and sides by ⅝". Spread glue evenly over the top of the desk, then carefully position the top for the ⅝" overhang on front and sides. Clamp it securely in place as in Fig. 23, and allow the glue to dry completely.

# *Drop-down door construction*

The drop-down front for this desk is basic frame-and-panel construction with two *stiles* (the two vertical pieces running the entire height of the door), and two *rails* (the two horizontal pieces that fit between the stiles). All four of these components are grooved on the inner edge to accept the panel, while the two rails have a short tenon that mounts into the stile grooves.

Begin by cutting a ¼"-wide groove ⅜" deep into the inner edge of all four workpieces the same way we did for both the Ammo Box and Hardtack Crate projects earlier in the book. Now cut matching ¼" tenons on the ends of the two rails as in Fig. 24. I've used the router table for this, but you could also do the tenons on the tablesaw. As always, first use some scrap of the same size as your workpiece to get the tenon just right before cutting the actual workpiece. When sized correctly, the tenon should fit smoothly but snugly into the groove. Fig. 25.

Apply glue into the groove and mating edges on both ends of one of the stiles as in Fig. 26, fit the rails into place, and check for square. Then slide the stile onto the other ends of the rails *without glue* and clamp up as in Fig. 27. We don't want that second stile permanently in place yet, but clamping it up dry helps the frame remain square during clamping.

*Figure 27*

*Figure 29*

*Figure 28*

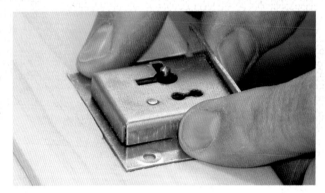

*Figure 30*

When the glue is dry, unclamp and remove the other stile, then slide the panel into place as in Fig. 28. The panel is designed to "float" in the frame, so don't use glue on the panel edges. Gluing the panel in place would prevent it from moving with seasonal expansion and contraction, which would likely crack the thin wood.

With the panel in place, apply glue to the ends of the remaining stile and clamp up the completed frame-and-panel door. Check for square and allow to dry thoroughly.

Cut hinge mortises on the bottom edge of the door identical to the ones you cut earlier on the mounting strip, and screw the hinges in place on the door. Then, attach the door to the desk temporarily to check the working action.

## Locking it up

Thicker doors (like those in your home) usually employ full-mortise locksets that are set into the center of the door edge. For thinner doors like the one on this desk, the most common type of lock

used in the 19th century, as now, was a half-mortise lock. The one I'm using here is brass, but plain steel locks were just as common during the period. This lock is ⅜" thick, about perfect for a door ⅝" thick. I chose a lock that measures 1½" x 2", but one a bit smaller or larger would be fine. Try not to get much thicker than ⅜"; a lock of ⁷⁄₁₆" is about the thickest a door of ⅝" can take. As the name implies, the lock is mortised on one side only. This will be a two-step mortise; a very shallow outer mortise matches the thickness of the thin face of the lock, while a deeper second mortise in the center of the other one accommodates the lock mechanism itself.

Mounting the lock will be easier if the door can be laid flat on a worksurface, so detach it from the desk for now. Start by laying the lock even with the top-inside edge of the door and trace around it with a knife or sharp pencil. In most locks the key post isn't in the center, so in order to have the keyhole exactly centered on the outside of the door you have to mount the lock slightly off-center on the inside.

As with the hinge mortises you cut earlier, use your chisel to define the mortise edges, then clean out the waste carefully. (Fig. 29) Check the mortise

Figure 3-1

Figure 32

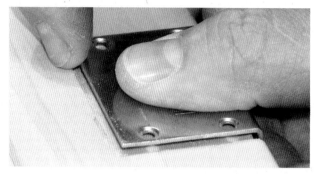

Figure 33

Figure 34

Figure 35

depth frequently as you work by putting the lock in place upside down until the depth matches the thickness of the lock face. (Fig. 30)

With the first mortise complete, lay the lock adjacent to the opening and use a straightedge to mark the second mortise for the lock mechanism. (Fig. 31) Because this mortise is deeper, you can use a drill to speed up the process of removing most of the waste as I'm doing in Fig. 32. A Forstner bit, with its flat bottom, is best. Drill very carefully, being certain not to drill too deeply. Clean out as much waste as you can with the drill, then go back to your chisel to remove the rest and square up the mortise.

The next step is to drill a hole for the keyhole. First, lay the lock in the mortise and press firmly in place as in Fig. 33. The lock won't nestle flat in the mortise because the key post extends from the lock mechanism; by pressing it in place the key post marks the wood, giving you an exact spot for drilling the keyhole. The hole need only be large enough to allow the key to pass through, but it's best to size the hole to match the opening in the escutcheon you plan to use (if any). Back up the door with a piece of scrap to prevent tear-out on the front of the door, and drill the hole. (Fig. 34) Test fit the lock and mark the door edge for the shallow mortise to house the top of the lock. This last mortise, cut the same way as a hinge mortise, will allow the top of the lock case to sit flush with the edge of the door.

Reattach the door and lay the desk on its back, closing the door for better access to the front. If you're using an escutcheon, hold it in place over the keyhole and mark the rest of the keyhole shape

with a pencil, as in Fig. 35. Shape the keyhole by removing most of the waste with a drill, then fine-tune the shape with a chisel, knife or round file. Attach the escutcheon with escutcheon pins.

The last step is to screw the lock onto the inside of the door and make the mortise for the lock's bolt. The best way to do this is to rub pencil lead or a bit

# A CAPTAIN'S GIFT

Not all officers brought or commissioned field desks for their use during the war. In some cases, dedicated troops commissioned desks from professional cabinet shops, and presented the desks to their commanders as a gift of affection and gratitude. One such desk is this one, which belonged to Capt. William Holden of Marietta, Ohio, and was presented to him by his men at New Bern, N.C., in 1863. The walnut desk measures 11½" x 16¼" x 23¾", and features outstanding veneer inlays on the outside of the drop-down front.

The desk is currently on display at The Castle, a museum in Marietta, Ohio (www.mariettacastle.org).

*(right) The outside of the drop-front has extensive use of crotch-walnut veneer, and intricate marquetry designs inlaid on the panels.*

*(left) The Holden desk features a green leather blotter, and finely crafted details on the inside.*

of ink over the top of the bolt and, with the door held closed, engage the lock so the bolt rises up into the underside of the desk top. This should leave a mark on the underside of the top you can use as a guide for the bolt mortise. Make a series of shallow drill holes on this mark to create a small slot. Most locks come with a small strike plate that can be added to the bolt mortise. Adding one would not be incorrect, but strike plates were rarely used in most desks and small cabinets.

## Finishing touches and variations

At this point you can consider your desk complete, although there are a number of things more you can do.

If you'd like handles, feel free to add them to the case sides. Handles can be simple wooden hand-holds nailed or screwed to the sides similar to those we used in the Ammo Box project, or can be metal handles of the type used on trunks. A wooden block attached to the sides with holes drilled for rope handles would also be correct. Avoid the common galvanized metal handles from your local home center, as these are not correct. On the other hand, handles or drawer pulls appropriated from furniture drawers correct to the period would be a perfect addition from our enterprising regimental carpenter.

A nice touch would be to add a leather blotter on the inside of the door, which was quite common for drop-front desks. You can see examples of this in both sidebars. Cut the leather to the exact size of frame opening, and glue it to the panel.

You can leave your desk without a finish if you'd like. A few coats of boiled linseed oil will darken the wood a bit and give it some protection from the elements, or if you'd like some color you can paint the exterior. An oil-based paint or milk paint would be perfect for this. A lot of desks sold by Civil War sutlers today are stained dark, and then coated with a modern polyurethane varnish—I recommend that you avoid both. No carpenter in the field would have bothered with stain on SPF wood, although a coat of shellac would not be incorrect.

The possible variations for a field desk are nearly endless. For one thing, you could make it exactly like this one, but flip it over before adding the hinge-mounting strip and top. The dividers and shelves would trade sides, while the drawer would be near the top. In this position, you can add a second drawer if you'd like, as there's no mounting strip or doorjamb at the top to block the drawer. Instead of a center drawer module, you can put the removable shelves or vertical dividers in the center and the drawers on one side or the other. In the project as presented here, we were limited in overall size by the fact that we utilized a hardtack crate for the desk carcase. However, if you made a carcase from scratch, feel free to alter the size as you see fit, giving even more options for varying the interior.

Finally, back up in the drawer section, I mentioned that I inset the center drawer module for a reason. Among the things a regimental commander would have likely kept in his desk were regimental or company books. These were thin, ledger-like books all officers used for record-keeping. There were a couple different types of these books mentioned in nearly identical regulations for both armies, with dimensions stated at 10" x 14" and 10½" x 14". Now, a hardtack crate of regulation dimensions measures only 9¾" deep, just a bit too shallow to store a company book. However, by insetting the center module (along with the dividers and shelves) at least ½" into the desk, I've allowed room for these books to be placed flat across the front when the desk is closed and stored. When in the opened position, these books can be slid into the dividers on the left with no problem. The point is, if you decide to make your own carcase, consider making it at least 10½" deep on the inside to accommodate a company book.

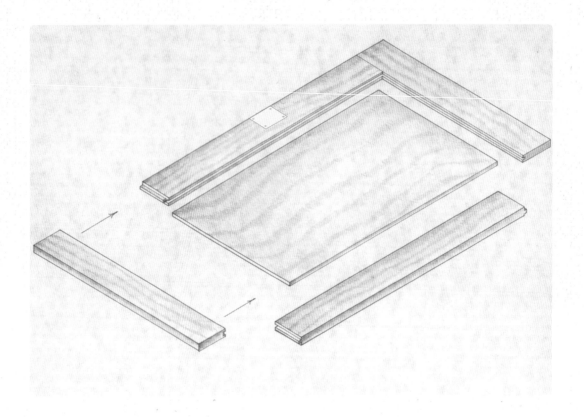

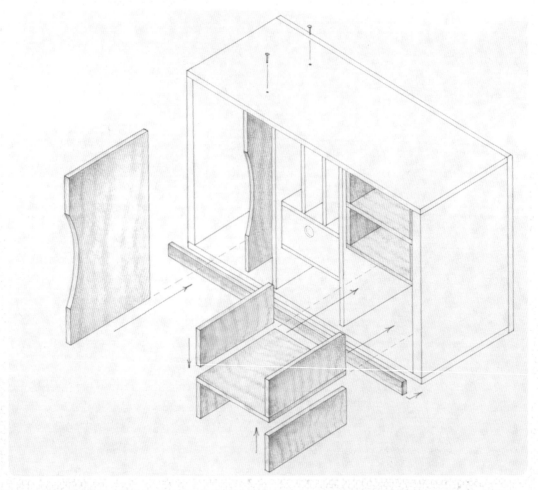

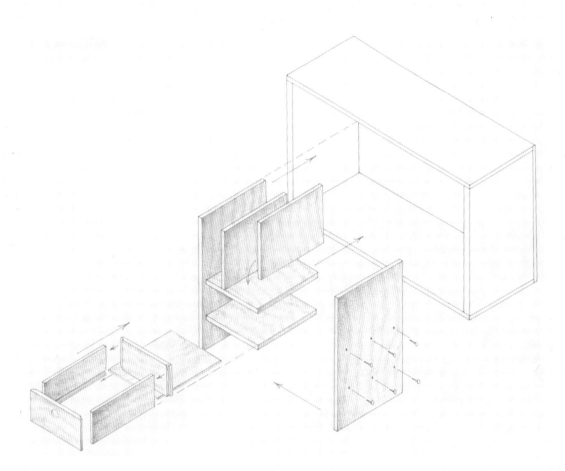

*Dr. Charles K. Irwin's tent with the 72nd N.Y. Infantry displays a fine example of a field desk. Culpeper, Va., 1863.*

# Chapter 11:
# FOLDING MIRROR

Sutlers like to market small items such as this folding mirror as "haversack stuffers." In truth, no Civil War soldier would have kept a mirror—or any other personal effect—in his haversack, as its purpose was to carry food. Authentic reenactors do likewise, and stow possessions in their knapsacks or bedrolls just as soldiers did during the war.

Still, personal items were necessary then and a small mirror was a boon to soldiers who shaved, and comes in quite handy today for their modern reenacting counterparts.

This particular style of folding mirror was a common design in the 19th century, as evidenced by the number of surviving examples. You can see a mirror identical to the one in this project on page 74 of *The Civil War: Tenting Tonight* from the Time-Life book series. I was lucky enough to find an original mirror a few years ago exactly like that one. The pivoting cover was gone, but the attachment point for the missing angled stop was clearly visible on my artifact as you can see in the lead photo.

## Through the looking glass

The best wood for the mirror case is a fine-grained hardwood. My original is made of cherry, so that's what I used, but maple and birch would also work well. Birch is primarily a Northern wood, while maple is common throughout both North and South. Figured maple such as tiger or bird's-eye would make a strikingly beautiful case.

It's a good idea to obtain your mirror glass before starting this project, as there's a great variance in sizes from suppliers. The glass in my original measured 2⅝" x 4", and I was lucky enough to find a source for mirrors of that exact size; I'll include the source in the resource list for this book. I've based all measurements for the wood components in this project on a glass of that size, but in the event that particular mirror glass is unavailable, not to worry. Original mirrors of this type varied a lot in size, too, so simply get a glass sized as close as possible to the one in this project and adjust the wooden components accordingly. Be extremely careful handling the mirrors, as few suppliers go so far as to dull the edges.

The mirror case is a sandwich. A ³⁄₁₆"-thick section in the center houses the glass. A ⅛"-thick bottom is glued on, and a ⅛"-thick pivoting lid is riveted to one end.

## *Cut List*

### FOLDING MIRROR

Overall Dimensions: $\frac{7}{16}$" x $3\frac{1}{16}$" x $5\frac{3}{8}$"

| Name | Qty. | Wood | Dimensions |
|------|------|------|------------|
| Top/Bottom | 2 | Cherry | $\frac{1}{8}$" x $3\frac{1}{16}$" x $5\frac{3}{8}$" |
| Center | 1 | Cherry | $\frac{3}{16}$" x $3\frac{1}{16}$" x $5\frac{3}{8}$" |

*See drawing and pattern on page 131*

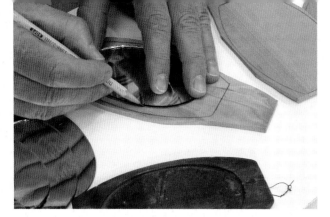

Figure 1

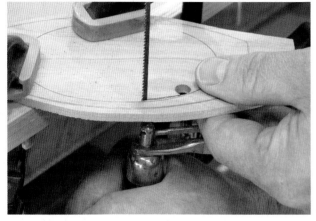

Figure 2

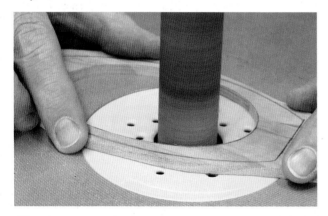

Figure 3

coping saw. (Fig. 2) If you're cutting by hand, clamp the workpiece to a secure surface; as you cut, you'll need to reclamp once or twice.

Sand the mirror cutout. The oscillating spindle sander in Fig. 3 is perfect for this. Check the fit of your mirror as you sand to be sure it fits the cutout easily.

## Glue-up and final cutting

Glue the bottom and center workpieces together to form the mirror case. Clamp securely as in Fig. 4, and allow to dry thoroughly. Notice that I've used a few lengths of wood as clamping cauls to distribute the pressure evenly. Since the glue will be completely unidentifiable in the finished project, I've used regular shop glue for this task, However, if you'd like to be totally authentic, use hide glue.

Now cut the angled stop from the lid workpiece. The best way to do this is with a miter box. First put a long piece of scrap inside the miter box and clamp both securely to a workbench or other surface. Now place the lid on the scrap and line up the cutline with the 45-degree angle guide on the box. With the workpiece lined up, clamp it to the end

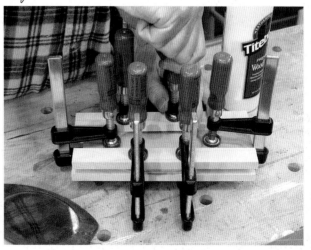

Figure 4

Start by tracing the outline for the case onto each your three workpieces, then trace around your mirror on the center workpiece as in Fig. 1. Also mark the cutline for the angled stop on the lid workpiece. I found it helpful to leave the workpieces a little long for now, as it makes them easier to handle and clamp.

Cut out the mirror outline in the center workpiece. This is a great job for a scrollsaw if you have one, but it's also easy to cut by hand with a

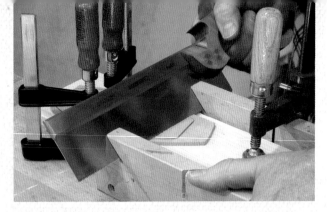

*Figure 5*

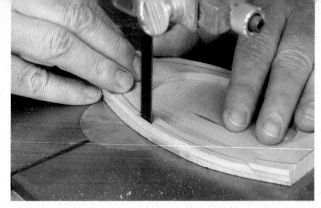

*Figure 7*

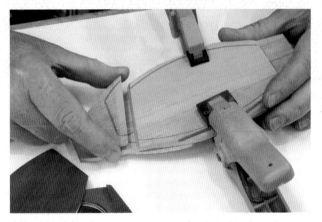

*Figure 6*

*Figure 8*

of the scrap to keep everything from moving, and carefully cut the angled stop free as in Fig. 5. To glue the angled stop to the case, temporarily clamp the top in place as in Fig. 6. This will allow you to line up the stop correctly. Glue the angled stop in place, but don't use too much glue on the front edge of the stop; you don't want to get glue squeeze-out on the lid. Once you have the angled stop glued and clamped into place, go ahead and unclamp the lid. Clean off any glue from the front edge of the lid that may have gotten on it while gluing the stop in place.

When the case is completely dry, cut it out on the outline by hand or with a jigsaw, scrollsaw or bandsaw. (Fig. 7) Note that I've made a continuous cut right through the angled lid stop as I follow the outline. Also cut out the lid at this time, but don't sand the edges of the lid or the case quite yet.

Drill a hole in the end to accommodate a small rivet. The riveting process is described in Chapter 2, so I won't repeat it here. The rivet can be located in the center, as I've done here to match my original,

or you can place the rivet in either of the corners. There are surviving samples that were riveted this way, so the choice is yours. With the lid riveted on, close the mirror tightly and sand the edges smooth.

Now is the time to finish the case if you wish. I gave the one here several coats of boiled linseed oil, followed by a coat of paste wax when it was thoroughly dry. Be careful not to get any oil or wax in the center where the mirror goes.

The last step is mounting the mirror glass. This can be done with hide glue, but once again this is something that is never seen in the finished mirror so I've elected to use a few strips of double-stick tape instead as in Fig. 8. The tape is much cleaner and easier to use, plus glue can adversely affect the silvering on the back of the mirror over time.

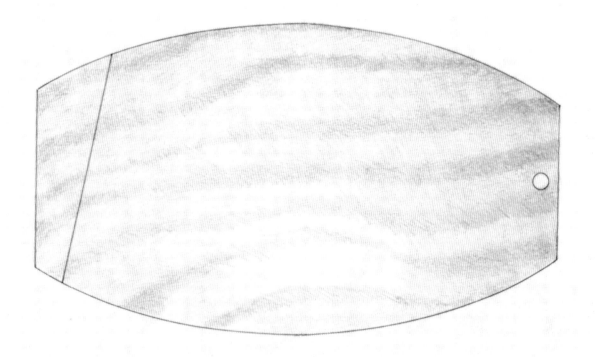

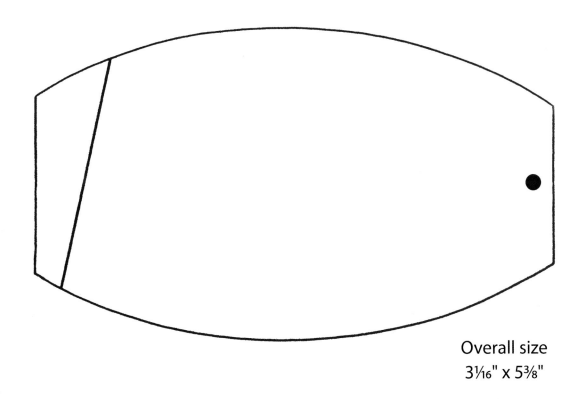

Overall size
3¹⁄₁₆" x 5³⁄₈"

*Capt. Cunningham of Gen. Thomas Meagher's staff at Bealeton, Va., in August 1863.*

# Chapter 12:
# TENT PEGS

No doubt about it, a tent peg (or pin, as it was sometimes called) is probably the least exciting project in this book. However, with these two styles of tent pegs I hope to introduce a bit more authenticity into a reenactor camp. A lot of reenactors use steel or iron tent pegs, probably because so many sutlers promote them. But the fact is that few foot soldiers would carry extra steel around on daily 20-mile marches, even if a ready supply of small metal pegs suitable for the typical dog tent or shelter half were available. Iron or steel pegs for officers' tentage may have been a little more common, but even then steel was needed for far more important uses, so wooden tent pegs were more likely.

For the privates, even carrying wooden tent pegs wasn't common. Wood, in the form of small trees and saplings or from discarded crates, was fairly easy to come by when the army stopped to camp, so issued pegs—if a soldier had them—probably didn't last long before being tossed into the fire or along the roadside. It was easier to make pegs than to carry them.

I'll cover two types of pegs here—a typical issued peg, and a camp-made peg. While these pegs aren't appropriate for all scenarios, each is more correct than iron.

## Issued pegs

This tent peg—patterned on one that appears in the excellent book *The Federal Civil War Shelter Tent* by Frederick C. Gaede—would have been mass-produced on period lathes, and while the specifications for this peg do not appear in records for either army during the war, it is fairly typical of the era. A peg of this type was described in quartermaster records a few years after the war, and this logical styling had likely remained unchanged over the years.

Making this peg requires a lathe, and I'll assume you're familiar with the lathe and its use. If not, a good source for learning basic lathe use and technique is *The Woodturner's FAQ Book* by Fred Holder.

As with all spindle turning, your tent peg begins as a rectangular shape that's slightly larger in diameter than the finished spindle. For positive seating on the lathe, I like to cut a shallow "X" in each end of the

## *Cut List*

## TENT PEGS

Overall Dimensions: Turned peg—1" x 9½"; Cut peg—¾" x 1½" x 9½"

| Name | Qty. | Wood | Dimensions |
|---|---|---|---|
| **TURNED PEG:** | | | |
| Turning stock | 1 | Oak | 1¼" x 1¼" x 9½" (a) |
| **CUT PEG:** | | | |
| Flat stock | 1 | Poplar | ¾" x 4" x 9½" (b) |

**Notes:**

(a) These are dimensions of stock before turning; allow at least 1" waste on each end for mounting.

(b) Stock size for cut peg makes four pegs.

*See drawing and pattern on page 137*

Figure 1

Figure 2

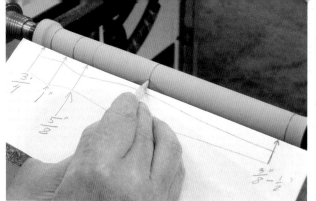

Figure 3

Figure 4

Figure 5

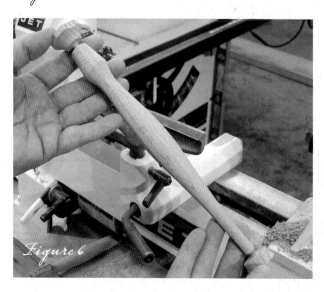

Figure 6

workpiece, as in Fig. 1. Mount the stock and set the lathe for a lower speed, then bring the stock to a round shape using a roughing gouge as shown in Fig. 2, or a scraper.

When turning spindles, I first like to bring the stock to match the widest thickness of the finished piece, so I turned the stock to a uniform 1" thick. With the lathe running, carefully transfer some key dimensions of the tent peg to the stock, as in Fig. 3. Kick the lathe speed up a notch and begin shaping the peg. In Fig. 4, I'm using a round scraper, but a spindle gouge would also be a good choice. As the peg begins to take form, check it frequently against your pattern; use calipers if you have them to get exact thicknesses at key points.

When you've matched the pattern to your satisfaction, use a parting tool to carefully cut thin connectors at each end of the peg as in Fig. 5, then remove the workpiece from the lathe. Note in Fig. 6 that I've rounded the tip a bit. Cut off the two mounting points from the ends of the workpiece with a saw or knife.

These turned pegs would have been made from hardwood only, as wood in the SPF families would be prone to shattering when hammered into the ground. The peg here is red oak, but any hardwood would be fine.

## Camp-made pegs

When the army was on campaign, the most common pegs made in the field were probably short sticks carved to a point with a pocketknife, and I'll leave those to your imagination. However, if the armies stopped for a longer period of time, the soldiers often took more care when making camp items, as already discussed in earlier chapters.

This tent peg is just one example of what a soldier might have made with a board and a saw. (In fact, that's exactly how this peg was designed—some years ago I needed some tent pegs, so I grabbed a piece of scrap and a handsaw and that was that.) Keep in mind that although I'm giving some specific dimensions for this peg, these dimensions are for example only. By all means make your own pegs any size you want based on the materials you have. I'll use a handsaw here, but cutting hardwood with a handsaw takes a bit of work so feel free to use a jigsaw, scrollsaw or bandsaw for this chore.

Start with a piece of 4"-wide stock. As with the turned pegs hardwood is best. I'm using poplar here, but you can use anything—just remember that pegs made with SPF lumber won't last long. Use a ruler to lay out four pegs, alternating their direction as in Fig. 7. Space them evenly, making the heads of each peg about 1½" wide and the tips about ½". The pegs shown here are the same length as the issued pegs at 9½", but anything longer than about 8" should do fine.

If cutting with a handsaw, mount your board vertically in a vise and simply cut the four pegs to length on the lines. (Fig. 8) Then remove the board

*Figure 7*

*Figure 8*

*Figure 9*

from the vise and cut across it to free the pegs. Cut notches on each side of the head, about 1½" or so down from the top, as in Fig. 9. If you'd like you can further sharpen the tips to make them a bit easier to drive into the ground by cutting angled points on the tips.

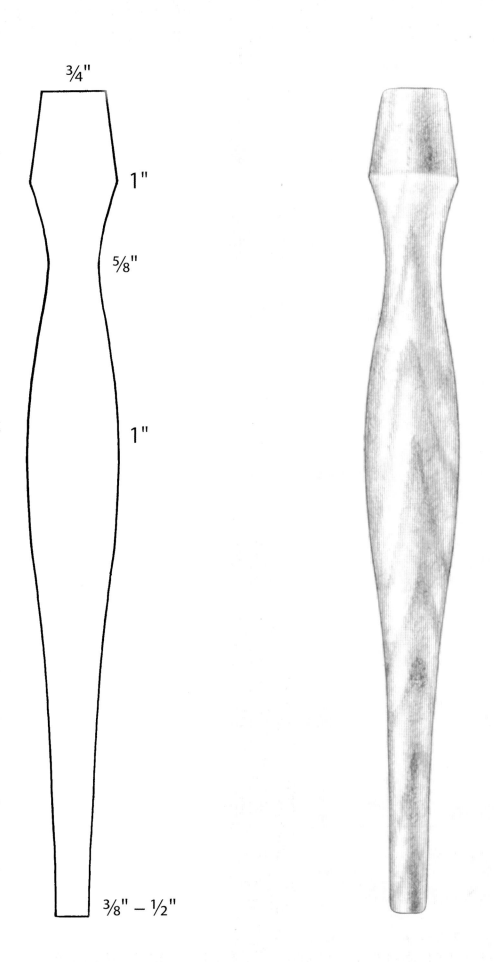

¾"

1"

⅝"

1"

⅜" – ½"

# Chapter 13:
# GAMES

For both Confederate and Union soldiers, army life in the field during the Civil War was made up of seemingly interminable boredom, occasionally interrupted by brief moments of unthinkable terror. The terror of battle is easy to identify, but when the soldiers weren't actively on the move they had absolutely nothing to do. Sure, there were jobs to be performed—water, firewood, foraging, and guard duties, for example, and regular drilling. But when not thus occupied the men had little to do except sit and wait for those moments of terror.

To make these times more palatable, the men engaged in reading and letter writing, or played games of all types. Gambling with cards and dice, while frowned upon by the officers, was common. Baseball (then called "base ball") was growing in popularity, and some regiments organized ball games when they could. And board games, just like today, brought hours of enjoyment. Among the more popular games were chess, checkers, backgammon, dominoes, and other strategy games.

*Soldiers play checkers on the deck of the* U.S.S. Monitor *on the James River in July 1862.*

## Cut List

# GAMES

| Name | Qty. | Wood | Dimensions |
|---|---|---|---|
| TURNED CHECKERS: | | | |
| Turning stock | 1 | Walnut | 1½" x 1½" (a) |
| FIELD-MADE CHECKERS | | | |
| Old Shovel Handle | 1 | Hardwood | 1¼ diameter (b) |
| FOX & GEESE: | | | |
| Fancy Board | 1 | Mahogany | ⅞" x 7" x 7" |
| Paddle Board | 1 | Cherry | ⅝" x 5" x 10" |
| Field-made Board | 1 | SPF | 1" x 4⅝" x 4⅝"(c) |

Notes:

(a) For turning stock, allow sufficient length for all checkers, at least ¹⁄₁₆" waste between checkers, and at least 1" waste on each end for mounting.

(b) This is the diameter of the handle I acquired, but any size is fine.

(c) These are suggested dimensions only; any size is fine.

*See drawing on page 149*

An entire book could easily be filled with 19th-century games, but let's take a look at two well-liked games of the period. Checkers remains as popular today as always; the other, Fox & Geese, although now lesser known, was a common pastime in its day.

Checker sets and Fox & Geese games were mass-produced in the 19th century, often using exotic woods and inlays in the game boards, and sometimes expensive materials like ivory, gold, and silver for the game pieces. However, because of their simplicity the games could also readily be made in the field. Both games were fairly light, and except for a full-size checkerboard they weren't particularly bulky. A soldier in the field might have carried one of the simpler commercial versions or one he'd made himself, so in this chapter we'll make both.

## Checkers

The game of Checkers is one of the oldest games known, with an Egyptian version called *Alquerque*—which used a 5-by-5 board and 10 playing pieces per side—appearing in carved images from 1400 BC. Evidence of similar games goes back even further. The version closest to the one we know today, adapted to a standard chessboard with 12 pieces per side, appeared in France about 1100 AD when the name changed to *Fierges*. In the centuries that followed, the French refined the rules a bit and the name became *Jue de Dames*, or simply *Dames*. This version spread around the world, sometimes acquiring new names as it went. In the 1500s it became known as *Draughts* in England, and a bit later as the common *Checkers* in America.

Commercially-available Checkers featured playing pieces that were usually lathe-turned. Some surviving samples have pieces made of a single wood species and then dyed or painted different colors, but more often pieces were made with contrasting dark- and light-colored woods. We'll do the same here, creating one dark and one light workpiece. Maple or birch are good choices for the light pieces; walnut, cherry, or mahogany work well for the dark ones.

Preparing the spindle workpieces for our version of a factory-made set follows the same procedure as the turned Tent Pegs in the previous chapter, so I won't repeat the instructions here. As with the Tent Peg project, start by bringing the workpiece to a uniform cylinder. I made my cylinders 1³⁄₁₆" in diameter, but Checker pieces of the period usually measured anywhere from 1" up to 1¾". (Larger and smaller checker pieces existed, of course, but anything smaller can be difficult to play with and larger ones are unnecessarily cumbersome.)

Cut the outside profiles of the individual playing pieces as in Fig. 1. This can be done with a couple different lathe tools, but a beading tool like the one shown in Fig. 2 makes for fast work, and ensures perfectly formed edges. I'm using a ³⁄₈" beading tool here, but these chisels are available in other sizes if you want a thinner or thicker playing piece. Go slowly with each piece, and leave a bit of room between each one, as you'll need to allow a bit

*Figure 1*

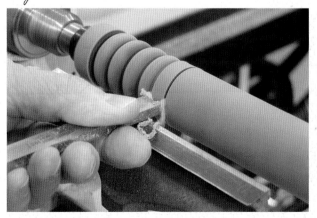

*Figure 2*

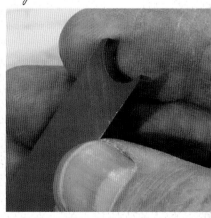

Figure 3

Figure 4

Figure 5

of waste kerf space when cutting the pieces apart in the next step. With the pieces all cut, sand the workpiece thoroughly as it spins. You only need 12 playing pieces of each color, but note in Fig. 3 that I've gone ahead and made some extras.

Cut the individual playing pieces from the turned spindle. In Fig. 4 I'm using the bandsaw, but a scrollsaw or fine-cut handsaw would work just as well.

Now sand the faces on both sides of each playing piece, as in Fig, 5. I've put fresh sheets of 150- and 220-grit sandpaper side-by side, sanding first on the coarse paper, then following up with the finer abrasive. When you've sanded all the pieces, give them several coats of oil finish, allowing the pieces to dry thoroughly between coats, then follow with some paste wax if you'd like a glossier appearance.

Checkers sets usually came without boards, as it was expected that most purchasers would simply use them with an available chessboard. A set of finely-made Checkers sold by themselves might come in a paperboard box or a thin wooden box similar in size and shape to a pencil box. A full Checkers game often came in a flat box that folded open to make a checkerboard, and you can see an example of one in the lead photo (these sometimes came with both Checkers and Chessmen). The average private soldier didn't always keep the original bulky boxes Checkers came in, tossing them aside as dead weight and transferring the playing pieces to a small sack that was lighter and easier to carry in a knapsack.

For a checkerboard, the soldiers most often drew a grid of squares on a scrap of cloth that could be rolled up. In some cases, the checkerboard cloth was used as the sack to hold the playing pieces by simply gathering the corners of the "board" and tying it closed with a piece of string, twine, or shoelace. Another option was to draw a checkerboard on the fabric side of a gummed blanket or poncho. They drew these checkerboards with ink, plain pencil, or even the tip of a charred stick from the campfire. If a can of paint was available, they could just dip a fingertip into the paint to draw the board.

Officers, of course, didn't have to worry about how to carry a small box, so they often had more elaborate playing boards or boxes that were packed with their other belongs when the army moved.

## Field-made checkers

Soldiers were nothing if not a resourceful bunch. Those not lucky enough to have brought commercially available games from home, found one while foraging, or maybe purchased one from a sutler, made do with games they made themselves.

A soldier required little to make playing pieces for Checkers. A well-seasoned straight tree branch of an appropriate diameter would work fine. A broken shovel or other tool with a long handle would be even better, and since my neighbor just happened to have a rusty shovel with a weathered, broken handle behind her house, with her permission I decided to use that as an example here.

To start, remove or cut the handle loose from the old tool, then just cut the handle into two-dozen thin disks. In Fig. 6 I'm using the bandsaw, but any saw will do except the tablesaw (not only will the tablesaw leave incorrect curved markings on the pieces, but once cut free from the handle the round disk can be kicked back by the saw blade; don't use a tablesaw). It's not necessary to do the cutting perfectly—many soldiers wouldn't have—so feel free to cut the disks without marking the handle first. Just eyeball the cuts, and they'll be close enough to the same size. As we did with the reproduction of the commercial Checker pieces, it's a good idea to make some extras.

The average soldier wouldn't normally have had access to sandpaper, so would have used any other available abrasive surface if he wanted to smooth his Checkers a bit. Any flat stone or brick, as I'm using in Fig. 7, would work nicely. To differentiate the playing pieces he would certainly have used paint if it was available, or might have just darkened one set with ashes from the fire pit. A quick-thinking soldier would have used a pencil to make different markings on each set. In Fig. 8 I'm putting X's and O's on the pieces, which not only makes them perfect for a good game of Checkers, but also for Tic-Tac-Toe.

Figure 6

Figure 7

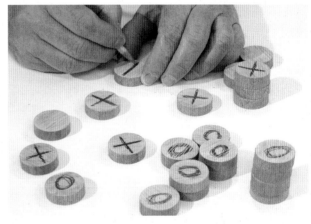

Figure 8

## Fox & Geese

Although not as ancient as Checkers, the game of Fox & Geese has been around for several centuries. One of the oldest versions, called *Tafl*, dates back to 4th-century Scandinavia. That original game branched out into a number of other games on the same theme: A two-player game where the sides are made up of unequal numbers, but where each side

# Getting it pegged

Where can you find period-correct game pegs? You can make your own, of course, as with the wooden dowel-and-bead pegs in one of this chapter's projects. But you really don't have to go to all that trouble. Any game supplier will carry cribbage pegs in numerous styles and materials. Also check your local craft stores, as they offer a variety of wooden pegs for arts-and-crafts projects.

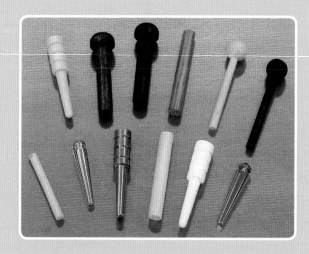

Pegs used in the 19th century were made of wood, ivory, shell and metal. They were lathe-turned, cast, carved and even crudely whittled. Pegs could be painted, stained, dyed, inked or just left plain. They could be simple straight sticks or could be intricately beautiful, and everything in between.

The bottom line is that there is no period-specific style of pegs that were used for games requiring them. Essentially, if you can find a modern-made peg that fits into a small round hole, as long as it's made of a period-correct material, then it's fine to go ahead and use it.

---

has distinct advantages over the other. The game evolved to a Viking version called *Halatafl*, which involved capturing corners on a pegged game board. As it began to spread across Europe, the game evolved further into a game of capture wherein a single predator attempts to remove all the opposing animals. Fox & Geese was the most commonly used animal pairing, but the game was sometimes also known as *Fox & Sheep*, *Wolf & Sheep* and *Fox & Hounds*, among other names. The original version of Fox & Geese used one peg to represent the fox, and 13 for the geese, which gives a slight edge to the geese (think maneuvering room in the early moves of the game). As a result, the number of geese was eventually increased to 15 or 17; the version with 17 geese was most common by the 19th century. See the sidebar for how to play the game.

For this project, you'll have your choice of making any one of three distinct styles of Fox & Geese. The first is typical of what might have been

manufactured in significant numbers, and is the fanciest of the three. These higher-end games often featured fine woods, carved details, and inlaid veneer or exotic materials like ivory or mother of pearl. The playing pegs were often metal or ivory, or may have been carved in tiny animal shapes. My octagonal design approximates a game board I saw years ago and is made of mahogany with a profiled edge. Etched lines enhance the playing surface. I ordered solid brass pegs to complete the set.

The second style would also have been mass-produced, but is more basic. Made of cherry, it has a paddle shape common to a variety of wooden game boards. The pegs are made with wooden beads and dowels.

The third version is a hand-made soldier's version. We'll save the soldier's version for last, but since the two commercial boards use similar construction techniques I'll describe them at the same time.

# Manufactured Fox & Geese boards

Start by cutting the boards to shape. For the fancy board, cut the workpiece to 7" square, then make marks on each edge 2" from the corners. Make a line across each corner on your marks, as in Fig. 9, and saw the corners off. For the paddle-shaped board, use the supplied pattern. The paddle board shown here measures 5" x 10", but you can size the pattern as you like.

Nothing needs to be done to the fancy board at this time, but sand the edge of the paddle board to smooth the shapes of the curves. An oscillating spindle sander is perfect for this; however, be careful if you're using cherry or maple for the board. Both woods have a tendency to burn—especially cherry—if you don't keep the workpiece moving briskly across the sanding drum. You can see in Fig. 10 that I must have forgotten my own advice and made a nasty burn on one of the inside curves. If you do the same, you must remove the burn mark—it's not only unsightly, but it's also an anachronism. They didn't use these powered sanders in the 19th-century, so a burn mark like this isn't correct. Fortunately, a minor burn like the one in the photo can easily be removed by hand sanding.

We'll use a roundover bit on the router table to form the edges of both boards (Fig. 11). Because

*Figure 10*

*Figure 11*

*Figure 12*

*Figure 9*

both of these boards have eccentric shapes, we'll be using the router table without a fence, allowing the bearing at the top of the bit to guide the cut. Be extremely careful to work slowly and keep firm control of the workpiece at all times.

Set the bit height so it makes a smoothly rounded edge and rout one side of the paddle board, then flip it over and rout the other side, as in Fig. 12, to get a fully rounded edge. (This profile, by the way, is called a *bullnose* edge.) Hand-sand the edge

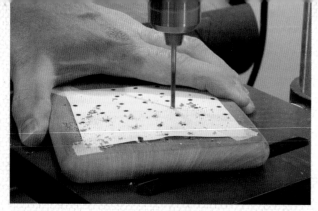

*Figure 13*

*Figure 14*

smooth to remove any milling marks created by the router bit.

With the bit at the same height, rout all eight edges of the fancy game board. Now raise the bit to expose the angled cutting edge at the bottom of the curve. You can see this cutting edge, called a *fillet*, in Fig. 11. Run all eight edges of the fancy board over the bit again to created a roundover with a small raised lip. (This profile, often used on table edges, is called a *thumbnail*.) Hand-sand as necessary to smooth the finished profile.

The reason we did this thumbnail profile in two steps is that a lot of material must be removed from the edge of the workpiece to create it, which is both difficult and dangerous to do on a single pass. By removing some material on the first pass with the bit set low, then raising the bit to finish the profile, the process is much safer and produces a cleaner cut.

Next is to drill the peg holes in both boards. Use the hole pattern provided at the back of the chapter, and scale it to fit your boards. For the

boards shown here, the pattern was 3¾" x 3¾" for the paddle board, and 5" x 5" for the fancy one. The easiest way to do this is to simply tape the pattern to your board and drill right through it using a ⅛" bit as in Fig. 13. The depth of these holes isn't critical, but somewhere around ½ to ¾ of the thickness of the workpiece is good. (I drilled ⅜" deep on the paddle board, and ½" on the fancy board.)

For the paddle board, add a ¼" hanger hole centered at the end of the handle

At this point, either of these boards could be considered done and ready for finishing. However, let's add one more detail to the fancy board by including etched lines between the peg holes. If you look at the holes, you'll see the pattern can be broken down to five overlapping 3 x 3 squares arranged in a cross pattern. Consider each of these squares as a unit, and use a pencil to create lines connecting the holes in each of the squares.

Lay a metal rule across the holes and scribe a line into the wood with a sharp knife as in Fig. 14. This can be tricky, so you may want to create a practice workpiece before cutting into the real board. Make your first cut exactly center-to-center on the holes, then move the rule just a hair to either side of that first line, and make two more cuts. What you should have is three cuts into the wood so close together that they create a thin groove in the wood.

I gave my paddle board several coats of BLO, followed by a coat of wax. You can leave the hanger hole as it is, or add a short length of knotted cord or leather if you'd like.

For the fancy board, I first gave it a coat of mahogany stain. This not only darkens the wood handsomely, but the stain pigment lodges in the cuts you made, making those etched lines really pop. When the stain was cured I finished the board with a coat of shellac.

I mail-ordered solid brass pegs for the fancy board, but for the paddle board I made my own.

This is easy to do with a length of ⅛" dowel and wooden beads available from any craft store. As long as they are made of American hardwood—most of these are made of either maple or birch—they're perfectly period-correct. Glue the dowel into the bead, seating the dowel so that it extends slightly beyond the bead, then clip the dowel to 1" to 1⅛" with a knife or diagonal cutters as in Fig. 15. When the glue is dry, sand the bit of extended dowel flush with the bead, and sand the clipped

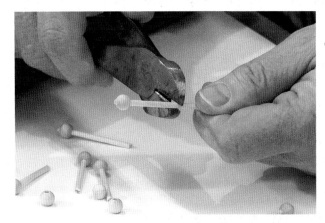

*Figure 15*

# RULES OF FOX & GEESE

It's difficult to list a definitive set of rules for Fox & Geese: There are so many versions. However, the goal is always the same. If the player controlling the Geese can surround the Fox so he can't move, that player wins. If the player controlling the Fox can eliminate Geese to the point where they can no longer hem him in, that player wins.

In the original game there were 13 Geese and one Fox, and everybody could move in any direction—left, right, forward, backward and diagonally. This early version of the game gave the Geese an advantage, so by the late 18th and early 19th centuries most versions of the game had increased the number of Geese to 15 or 17. At about the same time, although the Fox could still continue to move in any direction the Geese could no longer move backward.

Basic game play is the same in all versions. All the Geese are arranged on one side of the board. The Fox goes in the center hole. Geese go first in the 13-peg version, the Fox goes first in 15- and 17-peg versions. The Geese immediately try to surround the Fox, while the Fox captures Geese. The Fox does this by jumping over a Goose Checkers-style into an adjacent empty square (he can capture multiple Geese if the peg arrangement has empty holes

behind enough of them). In early versions the Fox was required to capture a Goose if he could; later versions relaxed this rule.

Variations: In versions where the Geese move in one direction only, the Fox can be declared the winner if he can break through and get behind all the Geese. The player controlling the Fox can place his peg anywhere to start the game. First move is decided by coin toss. Movement restricted to travel along etched lines only. In the 17-Geese version, Geese may not move diagonally.

I've played all the versions I've listed here, and with the exception of the original version where 13 Geese can move in any direction (and clearly win most of the time), I've been able to tell little difference in game play.

## SOLITAIRE

With some extra pegs, you can also use the Fox & Geese game board to play another game. In Solitaire, place a peg into every hole except the center hole (you'll need 32 pegs). Now, start jumping and removing pegs until there's only one peg left on the board. Strict rules call for that last peg to end up in the center hole, but it's often a challenge just to have one peg left when not even trying for that center spot. Good luck.

end square. The pegs can be oiled, dyed, painted, colored with ink or just left plain. The one peg used to represent the fox, however, should contrast in some way with the geese pegs.

## Field-made Fox & Geese

Soldiers could make their own version of Fox & Geese quite easily with a minimum of tools and materials. As an example, I've made the one shown here using only what a soldier might acquire in the field.

For the game board I used the Bucksaw from Chapter 7 to cut a rough square of wood from a piece of 1"-thick scrap pine left over from the ends of the Hardtack Crate project in Chapter 4, as in Fig. 16. I then drew the peg-hole pattern onto the board by hand with pencil and created a rough hand drill by driving a 2½" nail through a small piece of wood that served as a handle (Fig. 17.) Using this as a crude drill, I bored all the holes for the pegs into the game board, as in Fig. 18., by twisting the nail into the wood. You probably wouldn't want to try this with a piece of hardwood, but in soft pine the method works quite handily.

Coming up with an appropriate set of pegs was even easier: I simply used a handful of 1" cut nails for the geese pegs. For a different peg that would represent the fox, a 1½" cut rosehead nail worked perfectly.

Figure 16

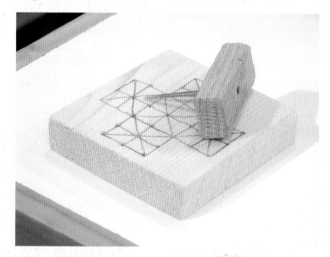

Figure 17

Figure 18

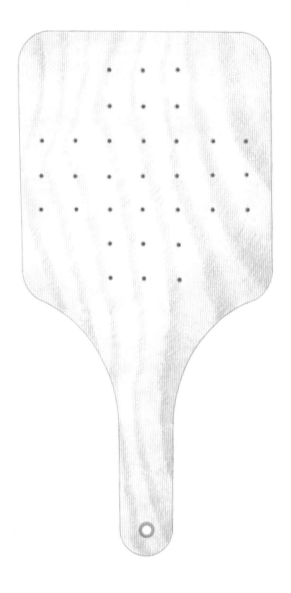

*Confederate reenactors play a game of cards to pass the time during*
*Moorpark Civil War Days in 2008, at Moorpark, Calif.*

# Chapter 14:
# CANDLE LANTERN

Candles have been a main source of lighting for centuries, with candlesticks, candelabras, sconces, and chandeliers common for indoor use. However, for use outdoors, in barns or stables, hung outside taverns and, yes, in Civil War camps, an enclosure of some sort to shield the open flame against wind was a must. A lantern served this purpose well, and could take just about any form. As long as you had a containment for the candle, some means of accessing the candle, a shield that allowed light out but not the wind in, and a handle of some sort to carry it, the designs and materials to make it were secondary.

Tin lanterns with punched designs or fitted glass panels were common before the war, as were wooden lanterns. However, with the coming of the war two things changed: The first was that metal was badly needed elsewhere for the manufacture of war goods. The second was that thousands upon thousands of men were suddenly living outdoors in tents, and all of them had a need for light. Wooden lanterns may have been common before, but now they were everywhere.

These lanterns were simple affairs and shared two common characteristics—a top and bottom plate that defined the shape of the lantern, and grooved posts between the plates that held panes of glass. Beyond those two characteristics, however, every other detail was variable. Four posts was the most common number, but I've seen museum examples of hexagonal lanterns with six grooved posts. Some had a glazed door that swung open on small metal or leather hinges to give access to the inside of the lantern. Others, like the one in this project, had a slot in the top plate that allowed one pane of glass to be slid out for access.

With mass production becoming more common, some lanterns were made in quantity during the mid-1800s. But because of their small size and simple construction, they were still most often made by local carpenters or blacksmiths. As a result, even though the basic design remained functionally the same, every other aspect of the construction tended to vary with the whims of—or materials available to—the builders. So as long as you stick with period materials, feel free to customize this project any way you like; it'll still be a period-correct reproduction.

As with the Camp Stool in Chapter 8, wooden candle lanterns are among the most ubiquitous of Civil War items in reenacting. There's hardly a sutler that doesn't sell them and, as with those camp stools, they all look

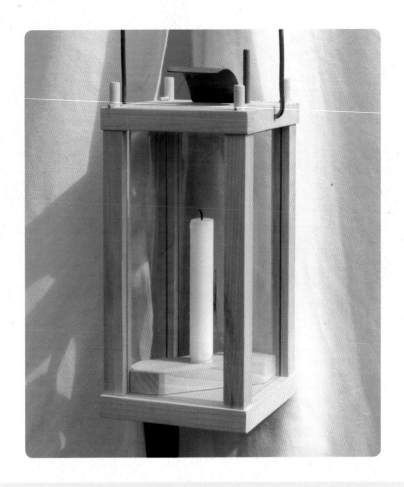

## *Cut List*

## CANDLE LANTERN

Overall Dimensions: 5½" x 5½" x 11" (to tops of dowels)

| Name | Qty. | Wood | Dimensions |
|------|------|------|------------|
| Top/Bottom Plates | 2 | Poplar | ¾" x 5½" x 5½" |
| Posts | 4 | Poplar | ¾" x ¾" x 9¹⁄₁₆" |
| Top Post Dowel Pins | 4 | Maple/Birch | ⅜" x 2¼" |
| Bottom Post Dowel Pins | 4 | Maple/Birch | ⅜" x 1" |
| Post Locking Pins | 4 | Maple/Birch | ⅛" x 1" |
| Candle Base | 1 | Poplar | ¾" x 2" x 5½" |
| Candle Pull Handle | 1 | Maple/Birch | ¼" x 11" |

**Additional Materials:**
Wire for carrying handle, 18"–24" long (brass, copper, steel, tin)
Pliable metal stock for heat deflector, 2" x 3¾" (brass, copper, tin)
Single-strength glass, 4 pieces 4" x 9"

*See drawings on pages 158 and 159*

exactly alike. Original lanterns were made of any locally available wood, but sutlers seem limited to offering them in either pine or oak. For that reason, if you plan to use your lantern for reenacting I urge you use any other type of wood. Hardwood is best, as it resists warping and cracking better than anything in the SPF families. I've used poplar for the lantern here, but cherry, walnut, maple, or any other hardwood is fine.

This project utilizes dowel joinery, a common technique used for centuries to create simple, yet strong butt joints. (It's still used frequently today, especially for ready-to-assemble furniture.) The four posts are drilled top and bottom to accept short dowels—usually called *pins* in this usage—which are set into matching holes in the top and bottom plates. This method makes for very fast assembly.

## Post time

You could cut the four posts to size first and then cut the grooves into them, but it's far easier (and safer) to do it in reverse. Running relatively short ¾" x ¾" posts through a tablesaw puts hands closer to the blade than they need to be, and handling small pieces on the tablesaw is always tricky. Instead, cut the grooves in a wider piece of stock first and you'll find the workpiece easier to handle. Also, by using a piece of stock long enough to make all four posts, you'll only have to make two passes to do all your grooving. It's a good idea to use a long enough piece of stock to make a few extra posts; in case you make an error drilling the posts in a later step, you'll have some backups ready to go.

The grooves should be cut ¾6" deep into the centers of two adjoining sides on each post. Assuming you have a regular-kerf blade on your tablesaw, set the fence exactly ⁵⁄₁₆" from the blade. Run your ¾" stock on edge over the blade, then run it through again on its face as shown in Fig. 1. Now flip the board over and adjust your fence

appropriately so you can cut off the ¾" x ¾" post on the other side as in Fig. 2. This will give you one very long grooved workpiece which you can then crosscut into posts 9¹⁄₁₆" long.

*Figure 1*

*Figure 2*

A standard-kerf blade cuts a ⅛"-wide groove, the perfect size for single-strength glass. If you're using a thin-kerf blade, check the groove using a piece of glass and adjust the width of the kerf as needed by moving the fence slightly and making multiple passes.

Drill ⅜" holes into both ends ¾" deep to accept the dowel pins that will mount the posts to the top and bottom plates. Center the holes ⁵⁄₁₆" in from

*Figure 3*

*Figure 4*

the ungrooved sides of the posts so they won't overlap the grooves and interfere with the glass. If you have a steady hand and a good eye, you may be able to do these holes with a portable drill, but you can guarantee perfectly vertical holes by clamping the posts into a temporary jig on a drill press (Fig. 3). What I've done here is swing the table out so I could clamp guide blocks onto the table edge that hold the post securely and squarely beneath the bit. I then swapped out each of the posts in turn to drill each end, assured that I'd drill in the same spot each time.

## Top and bottom plates

Cut a pair of 5½" squares, one each for the top and bottom plates of the lantern.

Drill four ⅜" through post-pin holes in each of the corners in the top plate, which will align the top and bottom plates for assembly. The holes should be centered ⅜" from the sides. Although the holes in the top plate go all the way through, the bottom plate has corresponding stopped holes in the same locations, so you might find it easier to clamp the top and bottom plates together and drill the holes simultaneously. Set your drill press so that the holes in the bottom plate will be ⅜" deep (Fig. 4).

Unclamp the plates, and drill a 9/32" hole through one corner of the top plate for the pull handle, with the center of the hole set 1½" from the sides. I like the hole at the rear left or right corner of the lantern, but it can be drilled in any of the four corners as long as the metal heat deflector (described later) doesn't interfere with the placement. The pull handle, which raises the candle for lighting and extinguishing, is ¼", but the slightly oversized hole allows the handle to slide up and down easily.

With a Forstner bit or hole saw, drill a vent hole 1½" to 2" in diameter in the center of the top plate. This hole allows for free air movement in the lantern, plus it ensures that there's no wood directly above the candle flame.

Draw a line ⅜" from the front edge of the top plate on a side that is *in line with the grain*, and create a slot ¼" wide and 4¹/₁₆" long centered on this line. (This should put the slot directly between the two front holes.) The front section of glass can be raised through this slot to replace the candle, or to clean the inside of the lantern. By making this slot in line with the grain, you have only two weak spots—one on either side near the end of the slot. If you make this slot against the grain, the sides will be strong, but then the entire front of the lantern ahead of the slot is weak; a single blow could snap the front off.

You can make this slot on the router table with a straight bit, or with a ¼" bit on a hollow-chisel mortiser. I've done it both ways before, but chose to

*Figure 5*

*Figure 6*

make the slot for the project lantern the way a local carpenter may have done it then: by drilling a series of ¼" holes along the 4¹⁄₁₆" length and then cleaning up the slot with a sharp chisel as in Fig. 5.

Cut the candle base and mark locations for the candle and pull-handle holes as shown in the drawing on page 159. The notches of the candle base will "ride" the inside corners of the posts like rails, allowing it to be raised and lowered smoothly. Drill a ¼" hole for the pull handle. While a ¾" hole will accommodate most candles, you can adjust the size of the hole to fit other candles if you wish. Both holes should be about ½" deep.

Flip the candle base over and hammer a ⅝" to ¾" tack through the bottom and up through the center of the candle mounting hole from underneath (Fig. 6).

Finally, cut all the needed dowels to length. Any wood species is fine, but maple and birch are the most common.

## Glass and assembly

For the lantern glass, use plain, clear single-strength panels cut to 4" x 9", available from any glass shop. (If you have a source of old glass with waviness or other imperfections, like an old window in a barn or garage, by all means use it! It'll be far more authentic than modern glass, which is as smooth as…well, glass.) While original lanterns were sometimes made with colored glass, the practice wasn't common except for signal lanterns, so if you're going for authenticity stick with clear glass. However, there are a number of examples of 19th-century candle lanterns that use three panes of regular glass, and a mirror in place of a fourth pane. Not only did the mirror panel help reflect light, but if the mirror was used as the sliding panel in the "front" of the lantern, a soldier could remove it to use for shaving and grooming.

Before assembly, it's a good time to give all those corners a bit of sanding just to break the sharp edges. The amount of sanding and surface prep you do depends on your intended use of the lantern. If you're going for an authentic, original look, rough edges and hand-tool marks are fine. Keep in mind, however, that these lanterns were often made entirely with hand tools, so tooling marks from circular saws, planers or routers should be cleaned up if you're going for authenticity.

Assembling is straightforward; as suggested in earlier projects, it's best to do a dry-assembly first to check the fit of all the components. Take particular note that the posts fit flush to the top and bottom plates. If not, shorten the dowel pins slightly to allow a tighter fit.

When you're satisfied all is well, glue the four ⅜" x 1" pins into the bottoms of each of the posts. Go easy on the glue; it doesn't take much for a

*Figure 7*

*Figure 9*

*Figure 8*

*Figure 10*

secure dowel joint. Using too much just creates a lot of glue squeeze-out.

Put a bit of glue into each of the four holes in the bottom plates and slip the posts into place. Make certain the glass grooves face the inside of the lantern and align with each other. Before the glue sets, slip the glass panes into place as you go to double-check alignment as in Fig. 7, and adjust the posts as needed by gently twisting them. While the glue on the posts sets, glue the pull handle into the candle base and check that it can be inserted and removed smoothly (Fig. 8). A loose fit is preferable, so if the base rides too snugly on the posts enlarge the notches a bit.

Glue the four ⅜" x 2¼" pins into the tops of the posts. When the glue has set, align the top plate with the four post pins, and slide it down into

position. You may need to tap it into place with a mallet as in Fig. 9, but if the fit is too tight, don't force the top—you could split out the front at the thin sides of the glass-removal slot. Wrap a bit of sandpaper around the top pins and twist a few times, then retry putting the top in place. Ideally, the top should not fit tightly at all.

When you're satisfied with the top's fit, remove it, temporarily take out the glass, and replace the top. Now drill a ⅛" hole through each of the top post pins as close to the top plate as possible, as in Fig. 10. Push the ⅛" x 1" locking pins through the holes to hold the assembly together. Since no glue is used on the top plate or the locking pins, the top can easily be removed for cleaning, adjustment or glass replacement by just slipping out the locking pins and lifting the top off.

## Add the hardware

To make the heat deflector, cut a piece of soft- to medium-temper brass to 2" x 3¾" with metal snips and smooth the sharp edges with sandpaper or a file. As you've probably guessed by now, I like the look of brass and use it a lot in my projects, but copper or tin would also work well. Since the metal you'll be using is relatively soft, you can form the deflector's rounded shape over any round mandrel, such as a pipe, then bend and hammer it to shape. Although the profile used here is a common one, it's not necessary to copy it exactly, as there was a lot of variation.

Drill a single screw hole in the center of the cover flat. Drill a pilot hole in the top of the lantern and attach the deflector with a single screw, which acts as a pivot point to swing the cover out of the way when raising the candle for lighting (Fig. 11).

For a carrying handle, cut a piece of heavy wire 18"–24" long and bend it into a U-shape. The handle can be attached in a variety of ways, all of them authentic. For thin-diameter wire (such as from a coat hanger), the best method is to form tight loops on each end with needle-nose pliers and attach the handle by driving a nail or screw through the loop. For heavier soft wire, you can also hammer the ends flat and drill holes for screw attachment. Finally,

*Figure 12*

*Figure 13*

*Figure 11*

*Figure 14*

you can also just bend the wire ends at 90-degree angles and insert them into 1"-deep holes drilled into the sides of the lantern top. You can see these methods in Figs. 12, 13 and 14, respectively.

## Variations

At this point, your lantern is complete. No finish is necessary—in fact, for utility use these lanterns were usually just left natural—but there are historical precedents for finishing your lantern pretty much any way you like. For a display lantern or one for home use, you can stain it, give it a coat of shellac, or even paint it with a faux antique look.

Feel free to alter the lantern dimensions in just about any way. You probably don't want to go any larger than the 5½" x 5½" footprint this one has, but you could easily scale it down to 4½" x 4½". Much less than that puts the candle flame very close to the glass. Likewise, you can alter the overall height as you wish.

You can also adjust the stock thickness to a degree. If you use hardwood for construction, you can go down to about ½" thick for the top and bottom plates by adjusting the dowel length and depth. (Keep in mind that the thinner the top, the weaker the sides will be near the glass-removal slot.) If you're using softwood, stick with ¾" or thicker stock.

Because of all the grooving and drilling they require, ¾" x ¾" material is best for the posts.

For the candle base, as long as the length remains at 5½" to maintain the notch locations, thickness and width can be anything you like. You can also delete the candle base and lifting handle completely. Instead, drill a shallow ¾" hole in the center of the bottom plate and raise the sliding glass to light the candle.

Some surviving examples of lanterns show no evidence of having a metal heat deflector, but for reenacting or in-home use I strongly recommend including one for safety reasons.

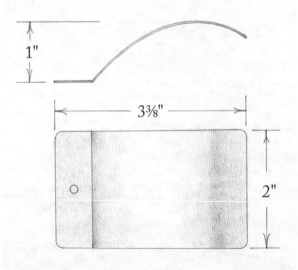

*Note that the length shown above is the deflector length after shaping. Length before shaping is about 3¾".*

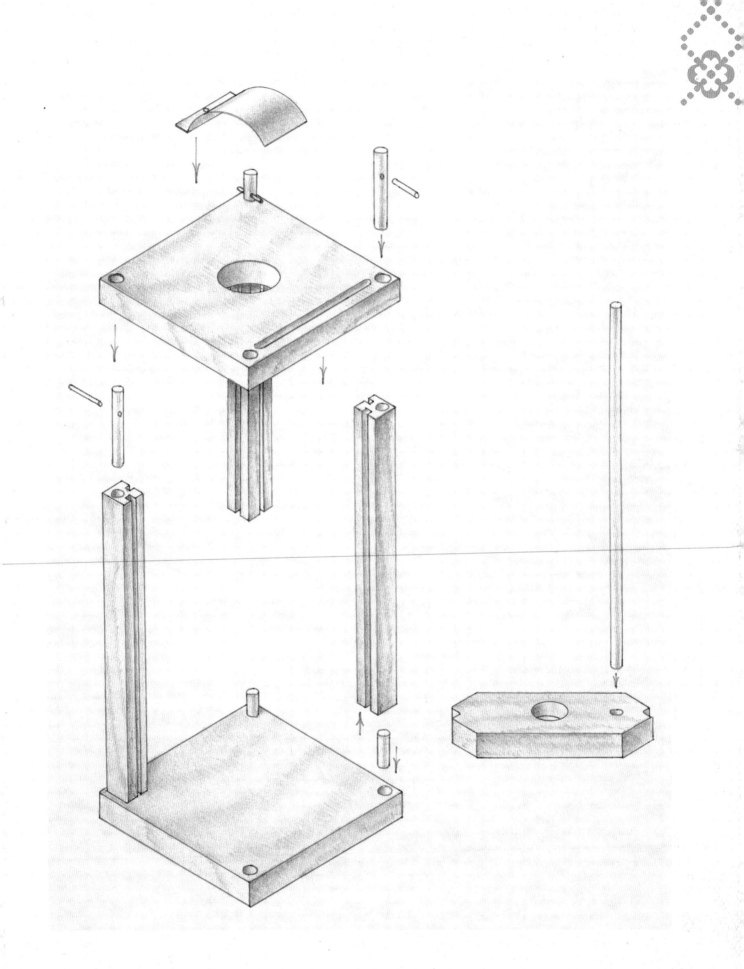

# More Information on Civil War Woodworking

## BOOKS:

Doing the research on the projects in this book was almost as much fun as building them. There are a lot of great books with information on objects from the Civil War period. What's listed here are books with extensive details and/or photos of potential projects, or for variations of the projects we've covered here. Of course, there are literally thousands of excellent books on the Civil War in general, so I've made no attempt to list them all. But here are some I found to be especially helpful to woodworkers:

*Echoes of Glory: Arms and Equipment of the Union* (Time-Life Books)

*Echoes of Glory: Arms and Equipment of the Confederacy* (Time-Life Books)

*Civil War Collector's Encyclopedia*, by Francis A. Lord (Dover Books)

*Collecting the Confederacy*, by Shannon Pritchard (Savas Beatie)

*The Civil War—Tenting Tonight* (Time-Life Books)

*The Federal Civil War Shelter Tent*, by Frederick C. Gaede (O'Donnell Publications)

*The Ordnance Manual for the Use of the Officers of the United States Army* (various reprint editions)

*The Ordnance Manual for the Use of the Officers of the Confederate States Army* (various reprint editions)

*The Confederate Field Manual*, (various reprint editions)

## WEBSITES:

As with books, there are too many websites devoted to the Civil War to mention them all. But here are a few of the best that are especially useful for research:

Library Of Congress Prints and Photographs Online Catalog, Civil War collection. **http://lcweb2.loc.gov/pp/cwpquery.html**

The Authentic Campaigner—An excellent site for reenactors who are really serious about the hobby. **www.Authentic-Campaigner.com**

The Civil War Reenactors—Another great site with tons of information for reenacting and general research. **www.CWReenactors.com**

The Camp Chase Gazette—The leading magazine devoted to Civil War reenacting. **www.CampChase.com**

The United States Civil War Center—Based at the Louisiana State University, this site is devoted to the interdisciplinary study of the Civil War. **www.cwc.lsu.edu**

**Civil War Historian**—A relatively new magazine specializing in the Living History aspect of reenacting. **www.CivilWarHistorian.com**

# Civil War Woodworking Resources

## LUMBER:

Just about all the lumber and materials used in these projects can be found locally. For general dimensional SPF lumber, plus some hardwoods (usually oak, poplar and maple), your local home center should be well stocked. Home centers are generally limited to 2-by (1½") and 1-by (¾") SPF lumber, and solid hardwoods of no more than ¾" thickness. For lumber of other thicknesses, as well as for hardwoods not carried in home centers (white oak, walnut, cherry, etc.), your best bet is a true lumber supplier. Also check local cabinet and millwork shops, as many deal in lumber as a sideline.

## HARDWARE:

Some of the basic hardware you'll need can also be found at your local home center. Brass hinges and round-head slotted screws are generally pretty easy to find in home centers and hardware stores. (When buying hinges, watch for things like company names or "Made In China" stamped on them; these would be anachronistic unless on the underside of hardware and hidden in a finished project.) Some home centers and hardware stores also carry cut nails, but not all. Unless you have a well-stocked industrial supply outlet near you, finding rivets of the correct type and material may be difficult. Rivets should be steel, brass, or copper only; no aluminum, bright or galvanized steel, or stainless steel. Most of the rivets you'll find at home centers will be "pop rivets," which are not correct for the period.

## GLUE & FINISHES:

Because it's invisible in the finished projects, I've used regular shop glue for most of the projects here. Hide glue would be more authentic if you're willing to take the time to use it correctly, but it's finicky. Although liquid hide glue is readily available, if you wish to mix up your own from granules you may have to go through a catalog or online woodworking supplier.

With the exception of the painted Ammunition Box project, all others not left plain are finished with boiled linseed oil (BLO) or shellac. BLO and canned liquid shellac are available at any home center or hardware store. Shellac flakes or granules are harder to find and you may have to mail order it.

## MISCELLANEOUS WOODEN SUPPLIES:

If you have a large craft store or perhaps a large fabric store with a craft section, you may be surprised at what you'll find there: small wooden parts, dowels, pegs, wooden boxes, and more in a variety of styles and sizes. Most of these items will be SPF, birch or maple, but check packaging or labels to verify that the wood is a domestic species and thus correct for use.

Unless you have a retail outlet of one of the major woodworking catalog suppliers located in your area, the rest of the items used in the projects will liked need to be mail ordered. Here's a list of suppliers used for the projects in this book:

Crafts, Etc.
7717 S.W. 44th Street
Oklahoma City, OK 73179
800-888-0321 x1275
**www.CraftsEtc.com**
• 2⅝" x 4" oval mirror

Horton Brasses Inc.
49 Nooks Hill Road
Cromwell, CT 06416
800-754-9127
**www.Horton-Brasses.com**
- Plain steel & brass table hinges
  (rule-joint hinges or drop-leaf hinges)
- Half-mortise lock, brass

Kennedy Hardware
10655 Andrade Drive
Zionsville, IN 46077
800-621-1245
**www.KennedyHardware.com**
- Plain steel slotted screws, round and flat head
- Slotted brass screws, round and flat head

Lee Valley Tools
P.O. Box 1780
Ogdensburg, NY 13669
800-871-8158
**www.LeeValley.com**
- Box tool
- Brass table hinges (rule-joint hinges
  or drop-leaf hinges)
- Hide glue
- Half-mortise lock, plain steel
- Shellac
- Slotted brass screws, round and flat head
- Two-part brass rivets

McFeeley's
P.O. Box 44976
Madison, WI 53744-4976
800-443-7937
**www.McFeelys.com**
- Slotted brass screws, round and flat head

R.J. Leahy Co.
1475 Yosemite Ave.
San Francisco, CA 94124
800-514-4106
**www.RJLeahy.com**
- Plain steel, brass and copper rivets; round
  and flat head
- Rivet washers

Rockler Woodworking and Hardware
4365 Willow Drive
Medina, MN 55340
800-279-4441
**www.Rockler.com**
- Hide glue
- Plain steel & brass table hinges
  (rule-joint hinges or drop-leaf hinges)
- Shellac
- Slotted brass screws, round and flat

Tremont Nail Co.
P.O. Box 31
Mansfield, MA 02048
800-842-0560
**www.TremontNail.com**
- Cut steel nails

A.J. Hamler is a woodworking editor and writer whose articles have appeared in most of the publications in the field, including *American Woodworker*, *Handy*, *Popular Woodworking*, *Wood Magazine*, *Woodshop News* (of which he is the former editor), *Woodwork Magazine* and *Woodworker's Journal*. He is the editor of *The Collins Complete Woodworker* published by HarperCollins/Smithsonian and, writing as "A.J. Austin," the author of two science fiction novels and numerous short stories.

An active reenactor for the last 15 years, A.J. is currently a member of the 27th Conn. Infantry, the 1st and 11th W.Va. Infantries, and Carlin's Battery D of the 1st W.Va. Light Artillery. Not surprisingly, his love of writing and interest in the Civil War have led to articles that have also appeared in *Camp Chase Gazette*, the leading Civil War reenactor publication.

A.J.'s affection for Living History isn't limited to reenacting; for several years he immersed himself in the 19th century to perform as a first-person role-player at Mystic Seaport in Connecticut, and portrayed both Union and Confederate soldiers in the 2003 movie *Gods and Generals*. When he's not out on the battlefield, in his woodworking shop or busy writing in his home office, you'll most likely find him in the kitchen where he enjoys gourmet cooking. A.J. and his wife, Sally, live in West Virginia on the banks of the Ohio River. Contact him at CivilWarWoodworking@ gmail.com.

*Officers enjoy a meal near Yorktown, Va., in May 1862 during the Peninsula Campaign. Note the hardtack cracker held by the officer on the right.*